The Awesome Power of God
Study Guide

Understanding The Tabernacle
And
Your Royal Priesthood

The Awesome Power Of God
Study Guide

Understanding The Tabernacle
And
Your Royal Priesthood

C.J. Thomas

Published by:
Sharing The Light Ministries
P.O. Box 596
Lithia Springs, GA 30122
www.myholycall.com

ISBN 13: 978-1456580155
ISBN 10: 1456580159
Printed in the United States of America

All scripture quotations are taken from
The King James Version
(Bold, capitals, and italics added for emphasis)

Familiar definitions taken from "Strong's New Exhaustive Concordance
of the Bible" Copyright 1992. Word Bible Publishers, Incorporated.

Illustrations from "The Tabernacle In the Wilderness"
Copyright © 1976, 1999 By Gerth Medien GmbH,
Asslar, Germany

Tabernacle furniture and book cover design by Sue Morrissey
Sue Morrissey Art & Design
www.suemartist.com

Foreword

This study guide provides revelation on the most important aspect of Christianity, which is prayer. The teaching by Jesus in Matthew 6:9-13, the Lord's Prayer, is a model or pattern for prayer. Revelation 1:5-6 states that by the Blood of Jesus we have been made *"kings and priests"* unto God. According to I Peter 2:9, we are a *"royal priesthood"* to show forth the praises of our God. Within the Tabernacle of Moses there are shadow pictures that show a relationship between the model prayer and our royal priesthood.

Understanding the true meaning and the correlation between the Lord's model prayer, the Tabernacle and our royal priesthood will bring in the Glory of God and His end-time harvest of souls!

The Tabernacle of Moses is one of the most spectacular creations that God has given to mankind. Just to give you a brief description of how important it is, let's examine the scriptures. Exodus 25:8 states that God told Moses to build Him a Tabernacle so that He could come and dwell with them. The Tabernacle of God made it possible for the holiness of God to dwell with man upon the earth. Hebrews 8:2 tells us that the Tabernacle of Moses is a replica of the true Tabernacle in heaven and that Jesus is the High Priest and Minister of that Tabernacle. The Tabernacle of Moses is a shadow picture of the life, death, resurrection, and total dominion of Jesus Christ. Every detail of the Tabernacle testifies of Jesus Christ, the Lamb of God!

Jesus is our great King and High Priest ministering in the heavenly Tabernacle. And He has made us king-priests; therefore we should learn how to fulfill this ministry. The truths in this book show that the Tabernacle of Moses is an awesome Prayer Pattern. And this Tabernacle Prayer will enable us to fulfill our holy calling to be king-priests unto God, our glorious destiny!

The Awesome Power Of God Study Guide

Table of Contents

The Tabernacle Of Moses

Ex 25:8-9

And let them make me a sanctuary; that I may dwell among them.
According to all that I shew thee, after the pattern of the
tabernacle, and the pattern of all the instruments
thereof, even so shall ye make it.

Introduction

Uniting In Prayer And Worship

What we are about to share with you has been hidden in the Word and the heart of God for such a time as this! This revelation is a gift from the Father to bless and unify the Body of Christ into His mighty invincible army. This **"corporate anointing"** will manifest the presence of God. Whether you are a part of the five-fold ministry, a seasoned Saint or a new convert in Christ, this revelation will bless God; bless you, and the world. It will also propel you into the Secret Place, the very presence of God!

We are God's end-time army, hand-picked, to bring in the final harvest and to fill the earth with His Glory. In order to accomplish this task, WE MUST UNITE IN PRAYER AND WORSHIP! To the natural mind that seems impossible as we look at the landscape of all the different denominations and Church doctrines. However, with God—ALL THINGS ARE POSSIBLE!

First Peter 2:9 tells us that we are a royal priesthood to show forth the praises of our God. Revelation 1:5-6 and 5:9-10 states that we have been made kings and priests unto God by the Blood of Jesus Christ. We have been redeemed by His Blood and given this wonderful and powerful ministry!

During this study you will see how the manifold wisdom of God has overcome denominational barriers. It has also overcome the gulf between Jew and Gentile, and every other obstacle to create His *"One New Man"* (Eph 2:15). The most spectacular element is the exponential multiplication (extremely rapid increase) of prayer power for the end-time harvest. Your royal priesthood enables you to pray for and on behalf of nearly 7 billion people! Yes, just one king-priest has that much power! Two king-priests produce about 14 billion prayers. Three king-priests produce just about 21 billion prayers. One can easily see *"The Awesome Power of God"* that will be released when the Church enters her king-priest ministry. Praise the Lamb of God forever!

More Than Just A Revival

This end-time Glory that will invade the earth is more than just a revival. We sometimes call it a "revival", because we don't really have the words to describe it! But it will be SO MUCH MORE and we need to be prepared! This move will be so great and so unlike ANYTHING we have ever seen on this earth! And because of this, our present methods of operation in the Body of Christ cannot contain it. In 1995, the Lord told us, at Sharing The Light Ministries, that we were called as a team of king-priest intercessors. We were told our mandate was to pray and bring the Body of Christ into a *"Paradigm Shift"* for this Glory. Not only were we trying to figure out how in the world we could accomplish that, but we had to find out what that word meant!

The word *"paradigm"* simply means *"model or pattern"*. The *"shift"* is that we have to *"shift back"* to God's *"original pattern"* and *"divine order"* of worship as outlined in the Torah *(Gen – Deut)*. The difference is that now the Lamb of God has come and fulfilled the shadow pictures in the Torah. We now have a royal priesthood *(king-priest ministry)* purchased by the Blood of the Lamb! And if we want God to DWELL in our midst, we have to come into unity and build and become a *"spiritual house"* for our Lord (I Peter 2:5-9). Our king-priest ministry, the Tabernacle Prayer Pattern and Lord's Prayer model are the powerful elements needed to bring us into unity. And this will be the FOUNDATION THAT WILL SUPPORT this end-time Glory! In other words, **the biblical heavenly pattern given to Moses** is the same one we need for HOUSING AND RETAINING THE MANIFEST PRESENCE OF GOD!

The Tabernacle Of Moses – Prayer Pattern

God, through Moses His prophet, commanded Pharaoh to let His people go so they may worship Him. Through God's mighty hand, the Israelites were delivered from slavery in Egypt. In the wilderness of Sinai, Moses was given precise instructions by God to build a Tabernacle, a place to worship and serve Him. In Exodus 25:8 the Lord said, *"And let them make me a sanctuary; that I may dwell among them"*. And God showed Moses the Tabernacle or Temple in Heaven and told him *"SEVEN"* times to build it according to the *"PATTERN"* he had been shown! The building of the Tabernacle was for the purpose of God dwelling among His people. He gave His people a way to receive atonement for their sins, and a method of approach to Him.

God, in His manifold wisdom, made everything within the Tabernacle to be a shadow picture prophesying the life and ministry of the Lord Jesus Christ—the Lamb of God. Glory to God, the Tabernacle not only stands as a testimony of God's plan of redemption, but also gives us the eternal model and perfect way to worship Him!

Let's begin our study of the Prayer Pattern with the linen gate that surrounded the Tabernacle of Moses. This is where we repent and enter God's gates with thanksgiving and His courts with praise. The first piece of furniture within the Tabernacle was the Brazen Altar where the animals were sacrificed. This is symbolic of Jesus, the Lamb of God, Who took away the sins of the world on the Brazen Altar of Calvary. We praise Jesus for shedding His Blood and redeeming us! Glory to God!

The second piece of furniture was the Brazen Laver. It was a basin of water where the priests would wash before ministering unto the Lord. At this Laver we thank Him that He is the Word made flesh and that we are washed by the water of His Word.

The next piece of furniture was the Candlestick or Lampstand. It is symbolic of Jesus, the Light of the world, anointed with the power of the Holy Spirit. At the Candlestick we thank Jesus that He gave us the gift of the Holy Spirit so we would be a reflection of His great light.

The following piece of furniture was the Table of Shewbread, with four corners, surrounded by a golden crown. It housed the twelve loaves of Shewbread, which were symbolic of the Jewish nation. The Table now represents the four corners of the earth and the Shewbread represents all the people upon God's heart. It is here we enter into our role as intercessors, standing in the gap and repenting for all men.

Next we have the Altar of Incense, which represents the fragrance of "true worship". We thank Jesus for perfecting our prayers and making them a sweet smelling perfume unto the Father. This allows us to go beyond the veil and enter into the presence of God.

At the Ark of the Covenant (Mercy Seat), we worship Father, Son and Holy Spirit and experience perfect communion. This is not only the perfect way to pray and worship the Lord but it will manifest "The Awesome Power of God!"

The Tabernacle Courts

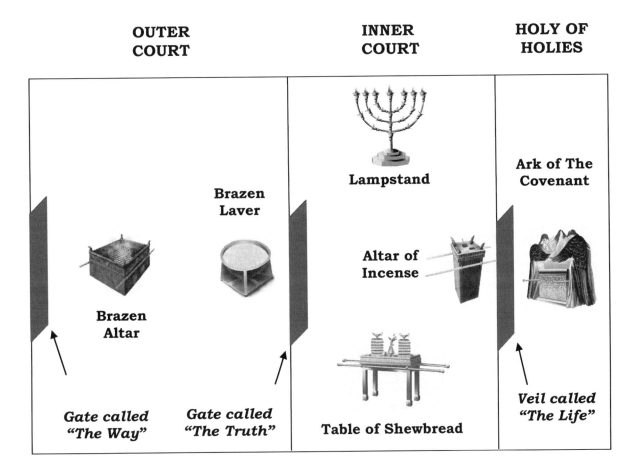

| OUTER COURT | INNER COURT | HOLY OF HOLIES |

Outer Court: "<u>The Place of Cleansing</u>" – In this Court stood the Brazen Altar of Sacrifice and the Brazen Laver. This represents cleansing by the Blood of the Lamb and being washed with the water of His Word.

Inner Court: "<u>The Place of Revelation and Service</u>" – The Holy Place housed the Golden Lampstand, the Golden Table of Shewbread, and the Golden Altar of Incense. These symbolize anointing and revelation knowledge, intercession for all men, and purging our hearts to bring forth true worship.

Holy of Holies: "<u>The Place of Intimacy</u>" – The Secret Place contained the Ark of the Covenant, which was the throne of God in the earth. This represents where we have fellowship and communion with the Father, Son, and Holy Spirit.

The High Priest Of Israel

Priestly Ministry

We Are A Royal Priesthood

It is a powerful truth that our Lord and Savior, Jesus Christ, made us kings and priests by His Blood. The next scriptures reveal our royal priesthood.

1 Peter 2:9
But ye are a chosen generation, a ROYAL PRIESTHOOD, an holy nation, a peculiar people; that ye should shew forth the praises of him who hath called you out of darkness into his marvellous light:

Rev 1:5-6
And from Jesus Christ, who is the faithful witness, and the first begotten of the dead, and the prince of the kings of the earth. Unto him that loved us, and washed us from our sins in his own blood, And hath made us KINGS AND PRIESTS unto God and his Father; to him be glory and dominion for ever and ever. Amen.

Rev 5:9-10
And they sung a new song, saying, Thou art worthy to take the book, and to open the seals thereof: for thou wast slain, and hast redeemed

us to God by thy blood out of every kindred, and tongue, and people, and nation; And hast made us unto our God KINGS AND PRIESTS: and we shall reign on the earth.

Before we can really understand our royal priesthood, it is necessary to understand the ministry of the High Priest of Israel.

The Precious Stones

Ex 28:21
And the stones shall be with the names of the children of Israel, twelve, according to their names like the engravings of a signet; every one with his name shall they be according to the twelve tribes.

According to Exodus 28:21, the breastplate of the High Priest contained twelve stones that represented the tribes of Israel. There were also two stones on the shoulders of the ephod that were inscribed with the names of the twelve tribes (Exodus 28:9-12). As New Testament king-priests, we bear the same stones. These stones now represent the unsaved, world leadership, the Body of Christ, and the nation of Israel. Isn't it startling that we have been given the responsibility to pray for physical and spiritual Israel, yet most of us have never been taught to do this? Most intercessors have been taught to focus on a particular situation or group of people, most likely, immediate surroundings. Our priesthood requires that we pray for ALL men. We can target certain people or situations ONLY AFTER we have fulfilled our priestly duty.

Intercession For All

I Tim 2:1-2
I exhort therefore, that, first of all, supplications, prayers, intercessions, and giving of thanks, be made for ALL MEN; For kings, and for all that are in authority; that we may lead a quiet and peaceable life in all godliness and honesty.

Another important aspect of the priestly garment was the robe. The hem of it was encircled with bells and pomegranates.

Golden Bells And Pomegranates

Ex 28:34-35
A golden bell and a pomegranate, a golden bell and a pomegranate, upon the hem of the robe round about. And it shall be upon Aaron to minister: and his sound shall be heard when he goeth in unto the holy place before the LORD, and when he cometh out, that he die not.

The golden bells were symbolic of the gifts of the Spirit (I Corinthians 12:8-10). The pomegranates were symbolic of the fruit of the spirit (Galatians 5:22-23). As Christians, we are out of balance when we do not have the fruit and the gifts operating in perfect balance. Without the love, character, and power of God we cannot be true witnesses. It is possible to operate in the gifts without development of the fruit in our lives. Additionally, it is possible to have well-developed fruit, without the gifts. Our Lord will judge us according to how well we have achieved this balance.

Holiness To The Lord

Ex 28:36-38
And thou shalt make a plate of pure gold, and grave upon it, like the engravings of a signet, HOLINESS TO THE LORD. And thou shalt put it on a blue lace, that it may be upon the mitre; upon the forefront of the mitre it shall be. And it shall be upon Aaron's forehead, that Aaron may bear the iniquity of the holy things, which the children of Israel shall hallow in all their holy gifts; and it shall be always upon his forehead, that they may be accepted before the LORD.

The mitre of the High Priest with the engraving, *"HOLINESS UNTO THE LORD"*, signified righteousness. God looked at the High Priest as the head over Israel. Through the holiness that was imputed to the High Priest, all of Israel was sanctified. This is the type and shadow of the Lord Jesus Christ, our High Priest, Who sanctified us through His holiness. We, as king-priests of the Lord, have been graced to share the holiness of the Lord and can also sanctify others in prayer, eventually leading them to a personal repentance!

The Power Of Our Royal Priesthood

Let's take a closer look at the priestly ministry of Jesus as the fulfillment of the shadow pictures in the Tabernacle. The high priest of Israel, on a yearly basis, entered God's presence with the blood of animals and made atonement for millions of people with his actions and prayers. Jesus, our model and forerunner, is the great King-Priest Who once and for all sanctified the entire world through His sacrifice and prayers. By the finished work of the cross, He was able to place His Blood upon heaven's Mercy Seat producing mercy for all mankind. **Jesus is now at the right hand of the Father ever living to make intercession for us (Heb 7:25)! And the manifold wisdom of God has given us a king-priest ministry to also affect the world!**

The way God counts and multiplies is extremely different than our thinking. The High Priest of Israel, a forerunner of Jesus, sanctified millions of Israelites through his prayers. And Jesus, our great High Priest, sanctified the entire world through His sacrifice! As a royal priesthood, the stones in our breastplate represent the living stones -- every person upon the earth! Yes, every king-priest has been given the power and responsibility to pray for about 7 billion people! In addition, priests are mediators between God and man. As priests we are not only praying for 7 billion people but we are also praying "AS" them! Let's just pause and think about that! Yes in the privacy of our prayer closet, as king-priests, we are releasing more prayer power than an entire stadium of people! **An EXPONENTIAL INCREASE IN PRAYER POWER will flood the earth when we have revelation knowledge of WHO WE ARE AS KINGS AND PRIESTS!**

Becoming God's Holy Habitation

As a royal priesthood one of our primary duties is to build God a house, or as living stones *"fitly joined together"*, BECOME HIS HOLY HABITATION. First Peter 2:5 states: *"You also, as living stones, are being built up a spiritual house, a holy priesthood, to offer up spiritual sacrifices acceptable to God through Jesus Christ"*.

We are called to UNITE AND BUILD OURSELVES INTO A SPIRITUAL HOUSE, a holy habitation in the spirit realm, by offering up spiritual sacrifices. The old covenant priests offered animal sacrifices. However, because the Lamb of God fulfilled all things, we have been graced to offer the sacrifice of praise, which is *"the fruit of our lips giving thanks to His name!"* Hebrews 13:15-16 tells us that with these sacrifices God is well pleased. Just as in the days of Moses when God told him to build a Tabernacle so He could dwell among them, God is asking us today to build Him a Tabernacle in the spirit realm and when we do, He will come and dwell with us upon the earth! And the knowledge of the Glory of the Lord will cover the earth as the waters cover the sea (Hab. 2:14)! Remember, He gave Moses a *"pattern or blueprint"* for building His dwelling place. Just because we are building a spiritual house with spiritual sacrifices does not mean we do not need a pattern also! And what better pattern than the *"eternal model"* for the worship of God, modeled after the heavenly sanctuary?

Through the Tabernacle, God has given mankind the ability to unite as "ONE NEW MAN"! Despite our differences, we can all enter our king-priest ministry and come into agreement upon and testify of what Jesus accomplished for us as the Lamb of God! As we *"testify"* of the Lamb of God, in agreement, His glorious Church will come forth by the washing of the water by the Word (Eph. 5:26:27)! Rev 19:10 states, *"....for the testimony of Jesus is the spirit of prophecy"*. So as we testify of Jesus, we prophesy God's Word and His will into the earth. And we become the "ONE NEW MAN", THE MIGHTY ARMY OF KING-PRIESTS, for which Jesus gave His life! And as His army of king-priests sending up spiritual sacrifices of praise, we will build ourselves into that holy spiritual habitation for God to dwell in our midst. Why is that important? Because it's going to take "HABITATION - NOT VISITATION" to evangelize the planet! Remember, He is waiting until *"we all come into the unity of the faith, unto the knowledge of the Son of God unto a perfect man, unto the measure of the stature of the fullness of Christ"* (Eph. 4:13). When we do this, the glory that Jesus walked in will be upon us!

The "One New Man" And The Prayer Of Jesus

Eph 2:15
Having abolished in his flesh the enmity, even the law of commandments contained in ordinances; for to make in himself of twain ONE NEW MAN, so making peace;

John 17:21-22 states, *"That they all may be one; as thou, Father, art in me, and I in thee, that they also may be one in us: that the world may believe that thou hast sent me. And the glory which thou gavest me I have given them; that they may be one, even as we are one"*. The Lord prayed that we become one and that He has given us HIS GLORY in order to unite. Looking over the varied landscape of God's children, it is easy to ask; "How in the world can we activate HIS GLORY to all become one?" Could it be that out of the manifold wisdom of God, He has made a way for us to do that?

In the next chapter, we will present a method or model for prayer that has the potential to unite the Body of Christ in prayer and worship. There are many types, methods, and models of prayer and we love and utilize them all. But what if a prayer that will unite Christians, Jewish Believers, and cross all other denominational barriers, is as simple as praying the "Lord's Prayer" model found in Matthew 6:9-13? For years, it has been prophesied that this last move of God would be brought forth through a **"CORPORATE ANOINTING", THROUGH ORDINARY CHRISTIANS!** It has also been said that the Saints would be empowered to release the end-time Glory and walk in it! And we would like to share with you a method of prayer that may accomplish this.

First let's look at the big picture. Ephesians 4 tells us that the five-fold ministry was given to equip the Saints for the work of the ministry. Verse 13 states: *"Till we all come into the unity of the faith, unto the knowledge of the Son of God unto a perfect man, unto the measure of the stature of the fullness of Christ"*. Yes, the Saints are to do the work of the ministry until ALL OF GOD'S CHILDREN ARE UNITED, PERFECTED AND WALKING IN HIS FULL POWER AND GLORY!

This vivid picture God is showing us is that His next move is so powerful and spectacular that it's going to take all of us to make it happen! The knowledge of the Glory of the Lord that will cover the earth as the waters cover the sea (Hab. 2:14), will take more than one leader, a Church or an organization. It's going to take the hidden power inherent within unity! To activate this power we must have true unity, which is not just the assembling of ourselves with one another. True unity is the unified Body of Christ in unity with the Captain of Heaven's Army – Jesus Christ! This unity will cause heaven to invade the earth and we will see the reality of *"on earth as it is in heaven"*.

The most stunning aspect of our king-priest ministry, uniting the Body of Christ in prayer and worship, is that IT IS EASY! In this study we have provided a long and short version of the Tabernacle Prayer. The full version you can pray in about 15 minutes, and the short version can be prayed in 3 minutes. We also show you how to design your own prayer for whatever time span you need, including an all night vigil. Long, short, large or small this Prayer Pattern will bless you and enhance whatever you are already doing for the Father. Above all it will unite the Body of Christ in prayer and worship. God will receive the unity and release the multiplication of prayer power and unity upon the earth! Glory to God!

The Vision Of Unity

In 1995, we received a vision of unity from the Lord. The Lord Jesus Christ was lifting up the **"Torch"** of the Abrahamic Covenant (Genesis 15:17), and all the nations of the earth were in one accord with Him -- in worship. This unified worship would be the catalyst for a worldwide move of God. As we began to seek the Lord about this vision, we were directed to His holy models or patterns set forth in His Word. And as a team of king-priest intercessors, we began to birth this vision into the earth.

At the dedication of the Solomon's Temple, as described in 2 Chron. 5:11-14, there was a powerful unity between the priests and Levites. They were in one accord and did not keep to their divisions, but **"BECAME ONE IN THEIR WORSHIP"**. They made **"ONE SOUND"** in praising the Lord and the manifest presence or Glory of God filled the Temple!

Could the powerful truths within our Royal Priesthood, Tabernacle, and Lord's Prayer, enable the Church to come into complete unity with each other and with heaven? And could this true unity produce the ONE SOUND our Lord is waiting for in order to release the "Awesome Power of God" in the earth? And then could we actually experience --- *on earth as it is in heaven*? We believe the answer to all questions is a resounding "YES"!

The Tabernacle And Lord's Prayer
Foreshadow The Ministry Of Jesus Christ

ARK OF THE COVENANT
Jesus the Carrier
of the Presence of God

7. THE HOLY OF HOLIES – THE PRESENCE OF GOD
For Thine Is The Kingdom, And The Power,
And The Glory, For Ever. A-Men.

ALTAR OF INCENSE
Jesus the Apostle
and High Priest

6.   PURGE YOUR HEART AND WORSHIP
HIM IN SPIRIT AND IN TRUTH
And Lead Us Not Into Temptation,
But Deliver Us From Evil

THE LAMPSTAND
Jesus the Light
of the World

**TABLE OF
SHEWBREAD**
Jesus the Bread
of Life

4. THANK GOD FOR THE ANOINTING
OF THE HOLY GHOST
In Earth, As it is in Heaven

5.   STAND IN THE GAP, REPENT AND
INTERCEDE FOR ALL MEN
Give Us This Day Our Daily Bread. And Forgive
Us Our Debts, As We Forgive Our Debtors

BRAZEN LAVER
Jesus the Word
of God made flesh

3. THANK GOD FOR THE WORD
Thy Will Be Done

BRAZEN ALTAR
Jesus the sinless Lamb
became the Eternal Sacrifice

2. THANK GOD FOR THE BLOOD OF JESUS CHRIST
Thy Kingdom Come

1.   REPENT AND ENTER HIS GATES WITH THANKSGIVING
Our Father Which Art In Heaven, Hallowed Be Thy Name

The Tabernacle And Lord's Prayer

Come And Take This Journey

We are about to take our journey as kings and priests through the Tabernacle. But first we need to understand the correlation between our king-priest ministry, the Tabernacle and the Model of Prayer given by Jesus, known as the Lord's Prayer.

Luke 11:1
And it came to pass, that, as he was praying in a certain place, when he ceased, one of his disciples said unto him, <u>LORD, TEACH US TO PRAY</u>, as John also taught his disciples.

In this account of the Model Prayer, we find that Jesus had just ended his prayer, when one of His disciples asked *"<u>LORD, TEACH US TO PRAY</u>"*!

First of all they knew in the ministry of Jesus He moved from ONE PLACE OF PRAYER TO ANOTHER --- WITH MIRACLES IN BETWEEN! So however He prayed --- they wanted to know! That phrase *"as John also taught his disciples"* is very interesting as well!

We know at least two of the disciples had been with John. We don't know exactly how he prayed, but we know that he preached *"<u>REPENT FOR THE KINGDOM OF HEAVEN IS AT HAND" (Matt 3:2).</u>* And he also said *"<u>BEHOLD THE LAMB OF GOD WHO TAKES AWAY THE SINS OF THE WORLD!"</u>* Now that's good preaching! No doubt he prayed in line with that. So keep that thought!

After being baptized and returning from the wilderness, Jesus began His ministry with these same words found in Matthew 4:17: *"From that time Jesus began to preach, and to say, <u>REPENT: FOR THE KINGDOM OF HEAVEN IS AT HAND."</u>* And these words were spoken by the <u>LAMB OF GOD</u>!

In Matthew 6:1-8, Jesus has just said, in effect, don't pray to be seen or engage in babbling and vain repetitions. Heathens do that, and don't be like them. The Father already knows what you need before you ask Him! So pray in this manner! In other words --- <u>THIS IS THE WAY YOU SHOULD PRAY!</u> And as a result <u>EVERY NEED WILL BE TAKEN CARE OF!</u>

Matt 6:9-13
After this manner therefore pray ye: Our Father which art in heaven, Hallowed be thy name. Thy kingdom come. Thy will be done in earth, as it is in heaven. Give us this day our daily bread. And forgive us our debts, as we forgive our debtors. And lead us not into temptation, but deliver us from evil: For thine is the kingdom, and the power, and the glory, for ever. Amen.

So if we want to cause the <u>KINGDOM OF HEAVEN TO INVADE THE EARTH</u>, we should pray <u>IN THIS MANNER!</u> And we should <u>BEHOLD THE LAMB</u> in all of His Glory! The kingdom of heaven is where God's rule is acknowledged and obeyed. And we are entrusted with bringing His kingdom to earth. And we can do this by praying the model prayer; beholding the LAMB of GOD, as we praise and worship Him!

Consider These "What If" Questions:

1) **WHAT IF** --- we all began to embrace the fact that we are <u>KINGS AND PRIESTS IN THE KINGDOM OF HEAVEN</u>?

2) **WHAT IF** --- <u>WE REPENTED EACH DAY</u> and began to <u>BEHOLD THE LAMB OF GOD</u> at each phase of His life, death, resurrection and total dominion?

3) **WHAT IF** --- this is the unity and oneness that Jesus prayed for in His Church: THAT WE BE IN UNITY WITH HEAVEN AND EACH OTHER?

4) **WHAT IF** --- this prayer is the <u>KEY TO THE GREATEST MOVE</u> of God upon the earth?

5) **AND WHAT IF** --- God allowed you to be born to the kingdom for a time such as this because He had confidence in you, that you <u>WOULD GET THIS and RUN WITH IT</u>?

THINK ABOUT IT!!!!

The Lord's Prayer And The Tabernacle

Kings operate in a government or a kingdom and priests operate in a tabernacle. **The Tabernacle of Moses happens to be the Government or Kingdom of God!**

The Tabernacle of Moses is the eternal model for the worship of God! When God wanted to dwell with man again, he showed Moses the Temple in heaven. And the Lord told him seven times to build Him a house on earth according to the Pattern he had been shown. The Tabernacle was a shadow picture of the life, death, resurrection and total dominion of the Lamb of God. **The Lord's Prayer Model is in the <u>EXACT PATTERN</u> of the Tabernacle of Moses and is in fact --- <u>IT'S FOUNDATION!</u>** So we are going to take a journey through the Tabernacle and the Lord's Prayer and find out <u>HOW WE SHOULD PRAY!</u>

Pray After This Manner

In this study guide we will explain each section of the Tabernacle, its furnishings and their fulfillment in the Lord Jesus Christ. We will also combine the Lord's Prayer and scriptures into a prayer for that section. This will give you a complete understanding of the Prayer Pattern.

In Matthew 6:9-13, Jesus was giving instructions on how to pray. He said; **"AFTER THIS MANNER THEREFORE PRAY."** Jesus was giving us a model or pattern for prayer. This means that we should follow the points brought out in the pattern, not that we have to say those exact words. Prayer, *"AFTER THIS MANNER"*, is in the exact Pattern of the Tabernacle of Moses! **"Our Father which art in heaven, Hallowed be thy name"**, represents repentance and entering His gates with thanksgiving and His courts with praise. **"Thy kingdom come"**, represents the Altar of Sacrifice. Jesus, through His life, death and resurrection, brought the Kingdom of God to the earth. **"Thy will be done"**, represents the Laver (the Word) because God's will is His Word.

The statement **"In earth, as it is in heaven"**, represents the Golden Candlestick which is the anointing and power of the Holy Spirit. The Holy Spirit will cause God's will to be done on earth as it is in heaven. **"Give us this day our daily bread, And forgive our debts as we forgive our debtors"**, represents the Table of Shewbread. This is where we repent for the world, spiritually receive communion, and intercede. We, as king-priests, must stand in the gap and repent for all men so God can bring blessing and not judgment. **"And lead us not into temptation, but deliver us from evil"** represents the Altar of Incense where we purge our hearts and worship the Lord in spirit and in truth.

"For thine is the kingdom, and the power, and the glory, for ever, A-men", represents the Most Holy Place where we see the manifest Glory of God and worship Him. Hallelujah! As you can see there is a DIVINE ORDER of prayer that God desires. The Pattern of the Tabernacle of Moses and the instruction by Jesus to pray *"after this manner"*, are in perfect harmony and clearly show divine order!

Jesus Is The Tabernacle

John 14:1-6
Let not your heart be troubled: ye believe in God, believe also in me. In my Father's house there are many mansions: if it were not so, I would have told you. I go to prepare a place for you. And if I go and prepare a place for you, I will come again, and receive you unto myself; that where I am, there ye may be also. And wither I go ye know, and the way ye know. THOMAS SAITH UNTO HIM, LORD, WE KNOW NOT WITHER THOU GOEST; AND HOW CAN WE KNOW THE WAY? JESUS SAITH UNTO HIM, I AM THE WAY, THE TRUTH, AND THE LIFE: NO MAN COMETH UNTO THE FATHER, BUT BY ME.

Jesus was telling his disciples that He was going to His Father's house and would prepare a place *(dwelling place)* for them. It is interesting to note that Jesus also told them that they knew where He was going and the way to get there! The answer of Jesus in verse 6 was in direct response to the question of Thomas; *"We do not know where You are going, and how can we know the way?"* In John 14:6, Jesus said, "I AM THE WAY, THE TRUTH AND THE

LIFE AND NO MAN COMES TO THE FATHER BUT BY ME". The Jews understood that He was speaking of the pathway through the Tabernacle. The entrances to the Outer and Inner courts and the Holy of Holies were known as the WAY, the TRUTH, and the LIFE. Jesus was saying I AM THE TABERNACLE!

He was also confirming that there is a DIVINE ORDER OF PRAYER that must be followed in order to get into the presence of the Father. In these scriptures, we have always thought that Jesus was just talking about taking us to heaven someday, and they can certainly be interpreted that way. However, Jesus was also saying that He has prepared a *"dwelling place"* for each of us where we can enter and abide in His presence, THROUGH PRAYER! We don't have to wait until we go to heaven to be with Him! When we enter His gates with thanksgiving and His Courts with praise, and continue to praise and worship our way into the Holy of Holies, we find ourselves abiding in God's presence!

The Stages Of The Tabernacle

The building of the Tabernacle was for the purpose of God dwelling with His people. He gave His people a way to receive atonement for their sins and a method of approach to Him. Everything in the Tabernacle was a type and shadow of the life and ministry of the Lord Jesus Christ. And God's ultimate purpose is to have a nation of kings-priests to come into His holy presence and worship Him.

The Israelites rejected their king-priest calling, and desired Moses to speak to God for them (Exodus 20:19). They did not want a personal relationship with God! This Prayer Pattern will give you the ability to have a personal relationship with God and fulfill your king-priest calling. While praying this Pattern your excitement will grow as you behold the Glory of our Lord and Savior Jesus Christ in every phase of His life, death, resurrection, and glorification. As you declare the Word of God in these areas, you will begin to see the "Word made flesh" or the manifested Glory of God in your life. You will realize, with more clarity, the power of the incorruptible seed of the Word of God to produce the Kingdom of God, in your life and the lives of others.

The front gate of the Tabernacle in the wilderness was called the "WAY". In the courtyard or Outer Court, the Brazen Altar and Brazen Laver were located. There was also a gate to enter the Inner Court, called the "TRUTH" and only the priests could enter beyond this point. In the Inner Court or Holy Place there was a Golden Candlestick, which illuminated everything. Next, there was the Table of Shewbread directly across from the Candlestick and the Altar of Incense stood in front of the veil leading to the Holy of Holies. The veil, which was called the "LIFE", guarded the entrance into the Most Holy Place or Holy of Holies, where the Ark of the Covenant stood. God's Glory (Shekinah) dwelt there above the Mercy Seat upon the Ark. Only the High Priest was allowed to go beyond the veil. He was permitted to do this once a year, on the Day of Atonement, to offer the blood of the sacrifice for the sins of the people. When Jesus said in John 14:6, *"I am the way, the truth, and the life: no man cometh unto the Father, but by me"*, the Jews knew exactly what He meant. **He was, in effect saying, "I Am the Tabernacle, the only access to the presence of God the Father".**

The Lord Jesus Christ is the fulfillment of the types and shadows in the Tabernacle. We must enter into the Gates, if we hope to find eternal life. We must also repent and accept Jesus Christ as our Lord and Savior, acknowledging Him as the Lamb of God slain on the Brazen Altar of Calvary.

After we have received salvation, we begin our prayer journey by repenting and then entering His Gates with thanksgiving and praise. At the Brazen Altar we daily acknowledge the power of the Lord's shed Blood – the awesome Blood of Jesus Christ! The Brazen Laver symbolizes the cleansing power of God's Eternal Word. This is where we are washed by the water of the "Word", Who is the Lord Jesus. The Golden Candlestick illuminates and reveals the power of the Lord Jesus Christ and the ministry of the Holy Spirit in our lives. The Table of Shewbread represents the four corners of the earth and the people for whom the Lord died. It is here that we enter our role as intercessors and intercede for those people who are on God's heart. The Altar of Incense represents "true worship" and it is here that we worship Him in spirit and in truth. This is the final step of the purging process that will allow us to go beyond the veil and enter into God's presence.

When Jesus died on Calvary, the veil of the Temple was rent in two, signifying that the most important step in life is to come beyond that veil into the Holy of Holies. In the Holy of Holies, stood the Ark of the Covenant, which housed the Tables of the Law, the Golden Pot of Manna, and Aaron's Rod. Jesus, the King-Priest-Prophet, was the Ark of God! It is God's desire that we become like the Ark, carriers of the presence of God with Christ in us, the hope of glory!

Many Christians stay in the Outer Court, or the Inner Court in their relationship with the Lord. They can still experience blessing, because the radius of God's presence is so great. But the fullness of blessing can only be realized by entering into the Most Holy Place, and into the arms of our loving *"Abba Father", "Daddy or Papa God"*. Our "Daddy" desires that we don't spend our time in the Outer or Inner Court. He is calling us to a face-to-face relationship with Him in the Glory realm. Praise God; let's answer that call! Dear Saints, in this realm, you have the manifested Word of God, His Glory, and His goodness. You will see your life changed and enriched in such a marvelous way.

This teaching is not intended to be an exhaustive study on the details of the Tabernacle. There are many great books that are available on this subject. This study is simply presenting you with our Pattern for prayer and fellowship with God. And we have also included the correlation of each section to the Lord's Prayer (Matthew 6:9-13).

As you begin to pray according to Pattern, you will be cleansed, purged, and will realize the importance of your calling as king-priest intercessor. You will notice the growth in your spirit-man because praying this Pattern is establishing the Word of God in your life that is already settled in heaven (Psalms 119:89). It is essential to understand that there is no greater force in the universe than the Word of God. The angels or ministering spirits hearken unto the voice of His Word (Psalms 103:20), not your opinions or ability to speak well, so please pray the Word of God! You will be empowered and learn how to bring "true worship" by worshipping the Father, Son, and Holy Spirit, in a new realm and with new revelation. So ***Come And Take This Journey With Me!"***

Come And Take This Journey With Me!

I bring repentance and thanksgiving,
Entering in by the *"WAY"*
For the Blood You shed for my sins,
I am so thankful each and every day.
The light of day or natural light
Is available, allowing me to see;
The Blood You shed on Calvary, for the world,
And thank God just for me!

The Blood that speaks of better things
Than that of Abel, even now;
It calls to the world in earnest longings;
"My children, where art thou?"
Then I enter into *"TRUTH"*, Your Word
Having washed and set me apart;
To be illuminated by the Candlestick,
So that I can begin to know Your heart.

The Light of the world, brings the light of the Word,
And I will glorify Your name;
And I know that in this, I am marked for life
And I will never be the same.
There's complete satisfaction as I receive
The "Bread of Life"; Lord I understand the cost;
So I bear the world upon my shoulders and heart,
As I bring intercession for the lost.

As I enter into the veil called *"LIFE"*,
Where the veil of Your flesh was torn;
As I bring true worship in love to You,
To Your life and purpose, I'll conform.
I worship You in the beauty of holiness;
I'll give glory due Your name.
And as I give You glory, honor, and strength,
You'll bring the promises I have claimed.

I no longer need natural light or candlelight
To obtain the promises You have for me;
Because now I'm in Your presence,
And Your goodness and glory, now I see!
Praise God, I have entered into the realm,
Where the God in Christ; becomes Christ in me!
This ageless truth hidden from the prudent and wise;
That Christ in me; is the hope of glory!

I've partaken of the Heavenly Gift,
I am a carrier of Your presence this day.
With the Word of God in my heart;
To blossom in fruitfulness, is the only way.
As I learn to abide in, walk in; and live in
The overflow of Your glory;
The world will know that I've been with You;
And I will be sure and tell the story!

And I'll invite them all to come with me,
And know what I have been graced to see;
All it takes is the willingness of heart,
To come and take this journey with me!

Daily Performing Your King-Priest Ministry

Heb 8:5
Who serve unto the example and shadow of heavenly things, as Moses was admonished of God when he was about to make the Tabernacle: for, See, saith he, that thou make all things ACCORDING TO THE PATTERN shewed to thee in the mount.

In Hebrews 8:5, we see that the Tabernacle of Moses was made according to divine order. It was a type and shadow of the heavenly Tabernacle, and foreshadowed the life and ministry of the Lord Jesus Christ. It is also our Prayer Pattern or method of approach into the presence of God.

Brass is found in the Outer Court denoting judgment; silver is found in the Inner Court symbolizing redemption, and gold is found in the Holy of Holies representing Divinity. We are not to spend our prayer time in the Outer or Inner Courts, but we are to go directly into the Holy of Holies—in other words, we are to "GO FOR THE GOLD"!

The Pattern is the most important aspect of the prayer **NOT OUR CHOICE** of scriptures, so please feel free to use your own favorite scriptures that apply to each section. The Word of God is inexhaustible so you can change often. However, even if you use the same scriptures, the revelation that God gives and the fellowship that you will experience will make it different each time. Use your Bible during prayer, or write your scriptures out. God is not concerned with whether you know them by heart or not. The important thing is that you are declaring the WORD OF GOD IN DIVINE ORDER.

The Pattern consists of three extremely vital stages that must be adhered to in order to be effective and get into the Secret Place of the Most High.

- The first stage is where you repent of your own sins.
- The second stage is where you are anointed and equipped to stand in the gap, repent and intercede for all men.
- The third stage is where you purge your heart and become a true worshipper unto the Lord and enter into His presence.

One cannot rightfully go beyond the veil into the presence of God, unless these things are taken care of first. Please understand that we are not saying that you have never been in the presence of God in prayer. All of us have gotten there on occasion, without this Pattern.

Those are the times that we cherish and remember as special prayer times. Those special prayer times happened basically by one of these three conditions: the grace of God, the Holy Spirit taking us there through our heavenly prayer language, or an anointed servant of the Lord taking us there. There is absolutely nothing wrong with any of these ways, however they do not give us revelation knowledge on how to return when we desire. God wants us to mature to the point, where we know how to get into His presence.

Also it is a wonderful privilege to approach the Lord with honor and respect as our great High Priest. If we were in the presence of an earthly king or royalty, we would follow proper etiquette or protocol. Why not honor the King of kings and Lord of lords when we enter into His presence? We need to let Him know that we have the highest honor and respect for Him by following His divine order!

The radius of God presence will bring great blessing in the Outer or Inner Courts, but you have not lived until you have experienced His presence beyond the veil! This is now available every time you pray, not just periodically. When you step out in faith and begin to worship the Lord in this fashion you will feel the presence of the Holy Spirit. It is His job to glorify Jesus and to bring you into all truth (John 16:13-14). Jesus also said the Comforter would teach you all things, and bring to your remembrance all things He has said! So just yield to Him and you will be amazed at how powerful your prayer time will become.

Do not concern yourself with the time element. God is so great in manifold wisdom that this type of prayer can be completed in one minute, or it can be transformed into an all night vigil. The Prayer Pattern provided usually takes about fifteen minutes. You can also alternate praying the steps of the Pattern with a prayer partner---or each person in a group can pray a segment of the Pattern to complete the prayer. You can do it anywhere or at anytime. As long as you do it according to Pattern you will experience the awesome presence of God!

Other Suggestions:

- Record yourself reading the full Prayer Pattern. You will be amazed at hearing how powerful you sound praying the Word of God.
- Play your recorded prayer often, praying along with it to get it into your spirit.
- Do not quote scripture references in the Prayer Pattern that are within parenthesis.
- Utilize the Short Prayer for quick access to God's presence.
- We also encourage you to create your own short prayer using the model at the end of this study guide. When you become comfortable with praying it, continue to add scriptures to grow your prayer.
- Bind Psalms 91 to everyone after completing major warfare.
- Once you are in the Secret Place, you are free to worship the Lord in the fashion you may be used to. For instance singing, releasing the song of the Lord, praying in the Spirit, soaking, declarations, reading the Psalms or releasing prophetic proclamations. Remember you are now in His presence so release your love to Him in sweet worship!
- Last but not least, enhance your prayer even further by using God's Jewish Names. He loves it! Jesus can be referred to as Yeshua (Our Salvation) or Yahshua (Our God is our Salvation). The Holy Spirit can be referred to as the Ruach HaKodesh and God the Father as YHVH or Yahweh!

The Gate – Repentance/Entering

Repentance

Ps 66:18-20

*If I regard iniquity in my heart, the Lord will not hear me: But
verily God hath heard me; he hath attended to the voice of
my prayer. Blessed be God, which hath not turned
away my prayer, nor his mercy from me.*

The Gate Called "The Way"

Repentance

Ex 27:16
And for the gate of the court shall be an hanging of twenty cubits, of blue, and purple, and scarlet, and fine twined linen, wrought with needlework: and their pillars shall be four, and their sockets four.

In prayer we must begin with repentance. In the Old Testament the priests were instructed to wash before performing any priestly duties, this was their repentance. If they did not heed this instruction, it would result in their death. Today we do not die physically (Praise God!), but our prayers do suffer a form of spiritual death – they are not as effective.

Ex 30:18-21
Thou shalt also make a laver of brass, and his foot also of brass, to wash withal: and thou shalt put it between the tabernacle of the congregation and the altar, and thou shalt put water therein.

For Aaron and his sons shall wash their hands and their feet thereat:

When they go into the tabernacle of the congregation, they shall wash with water, that they die not; or when they come near to the altar to minister, to burn offering made by fire unto the LORD:

So they shall wash their hands and their feet, that they die not: and it shall be a statute for ever to them, even to him and to his seed throughout their generations.

The word *"repent"* essentially means to be sorry and have a change of heart in turning back to God. When *"re-pent"* is broken down, *"re"* means back, again, anew and *"pent"* means up. This is where we get the word penthouse, denoting the highest level of a building. Therefore, when we repent, we return to the highest level with God.

Repentance is vitally important to prayer.

Ps 66:18-20
If I regard iniquity in my heart, the Lord will not hear me: But verily God hath heard me; he hath attended to the voice of my prayer. Blessed be God, which hath not turned away my prayer, nor his mercy from me.

1 John 1:9
If we confess our sins, he is faithful and just to forgive us our sins, and to cleanse us from all unrighteousness.

David's Repentance

Ps 51:1-5
Have mercy upon me, O God, according to thy lovingkindness: according unto the multitude of thy tender mercies blot out my transgressions. Wash me thoroughly from mine iniquity, and cleanse me from my sin. For I acknowledge my transgressions: and my sin is ever before me. Against thee, thee only, have I sinned, and done this evil in thy sight: that thou mightest be justified when thou speakest, and be clear when thou judgest. Behold, I was shapen in iniquity; and in sin did my mother conceive me.

David was guilty of adultery with Bathsheba and the murder of her husband, Uriah (II Samuel 12:9). David acknowledges both his iniquity and sin. Iniquity is also sin, but involves more of a "bent or leaning towards" sin because we were in fact born with a "twisted" sin nature. David asks to be purged inwardly and cleansed from both. According to the Law, he should have been sentenced to death.   Both sins carried a penalty of death. However, David asked God for deliverance from *"bloodguiltiness"* and his repentance reversed the death sentence (Psalms 51:14).   David, having a revelation of God's love and mercy, appealed to Him on that basis and his life was spared.   In Psalms 51:4, David declares that his sin was against God alone. This is a very powerful element of repentance. When we do anything to harm others or ourselves we are in fact sinning against God. Therefore true repentance involves the acknowledgment that we sinned not only against our fellowman but also against God.

God couldn't help but be touched by David's plea for deliverance and cleansing! David also asked not be cast out of God's presence and that the Holy Spirit not be taken from him. He then asked for restoration of the joy of His salvation and then promises to convert sinners to God.   David first thought of offering sacrifices for his sins. Yet according to Psalms 51:16, he knows God does not desire burnt offerings without true heart repentance. In verse 17, David goes on to say that a broken spirit and a broken and contrite heart are what God desires.   And when he brings these heart attitudes to God, only then will his burnt offerings be acceptable unto Him.

Ps 51:10
Create in me a clean heart, O God; and renew a right spirit within me.

Ps 19:12-14
Who can understand his errors? Cleanse thou me from secret faults. Keep back thy servant also from presumptuous sins; let them not have dominion over me: then shall I be upright, and I shall be innocent from the great transgression. Let the words of my mouth, and the meditation of my heart, be acceptable in thy sight, O LORD, my strength, and my redeemer.

When we repent, we should repent for sins known and unknown, those of word, thought and deed and secret faults. God is holy and He desires us to be holy in order to have fellowship with Him. The Psalmist says it best, when asking for the creation of a clean heart and the renewal of a right spirit within.   He then asks for that perfect acceptance in the Lord's sight by exercising the right words and right thoughts, to be pleasing unto Him.

The Gate – Repentance/Entering

Entering His Gates

Our Father Which Art In Heaven
Hallowed Be Thy Name

Ps 100:4

Enter into his gates with thanksgiving, and into his courts with praise: be thankful unto him, and bless his name.

The Gate Called "The Way"

Entering His Gates

Psalm 100:4 tells us to enter His gates with thanksgiving and His courts with praise, blessing His name. When we enter the Gate called "The Way" we hallow the name of the Lord. First of all we acknowledge He is our Father and we offer thanksgiving on that basis. We thank Jesus for being our Lord and Savior and revealing the Father-heart of God to us. We thank the precious Holy Spirit for being our Comforter, Lover of our souls, and our closest Friend. Most of all, we thank our Father for His grace and goodness in bringing us into perfect relationship with Him through the Lamb of God!

We then begin to hallow the names of the Lord. It would be beneficial to obtain a listing of the redemptive names of God. Below is a partial list. In the redemptive names of Yahweh or Jehovah there is great power. God will respond to us and manifest our blessings based upon our revelation knowledge of His nature and character. So when we hallow or consecrate His name, He will become everything we need Him to be!

Redemptive Names of God

Yahweh Tsidkenu - Righteousness

Yahweh M'kaddesh - Sanctifier

Yahweh Shalom - Peace

Yahweh Shammah – Ever Present

Yahweh Rophe - Healer

Yahweh Jireh - Provider

Yahweh Rohi - Shepherd

Yahweh Nissi - Banner

Our Father Which Art In Heaven, Hallowed Be Thy Name
(Matt 6:9)

Our Lord Jesus revealed God to us as our Father. We respond with thanksgiving for the goodness and favor of God. We begin to praise, exalt, and extol the name of the Lord. We can thank Him with scripture declaring the power, strength, and majesty of His name. Once we have hallowed or consecrated His name, we have established our foundation for thanksgiving, praise, and worship, throughout the Tabernacle.

Model For Creating Your Own Prayer

1. Repent
(Father I Repent And Confess My Sins)

_____
_____
_____
_____
_____
_____
_____
_____
_____
_____
_____
_____
_____
_____

Enter His Gates With Thanksgiving
(Our Father Which Art In Heaven, Hallowed Be Thy Name)

_____

_____

_____

_____

_____

_____

_____

_____

_____

_____

_____

_____

_____

_____

_____

_____

_____

The Prayer Pattern

Prayer:

1. *The Gate - Repentance*

FATHER I REPENT AND CONFESS MY SINS.

Father, have mercy upon me according to Your loving kindness and tender mercies and blot out my transgressions. Wash me from iniquity and cleanse me from sin. For against You and You only I have sinned **(Ps 51:1-4).** Father in the name of Jesus, I repent for every sin known, unknown, omitted, and committed. I repent for unforgiveness and I release and forgive all **(Mark 11:25).** I ask You to cleanse me from secret faults and keep me back from presumptuous sins; and let them not have dominion over me: then I shall be upright, and innocent from the great transgression **(Ps 19:12-13).** Father, I thank You that Your Word says in **I John 1:9,** if I confess my sins, You are faithful and just to forgive me, and to cleanse me from all unrighteousness. Create in me a clean heart and renew a right spirit within me and let the words of my mouth and the meditation of my heart be acceptable in Your sight O Lord my strength and Redeemer **(Ps 51:10) -- (Ps 19:14).**

The Gate - Thanksgiving
FATHER I ENTER YOUR GATES WITH THANKSGIVING.
[Our Father Which Art In Heaven, Hallowed Be Thy Name]

Father I praise You, hallow Your holy name, and thank You for Your love. Lord I praise You for Your mighty acts and I praise You according to Your excellent greatness. Let everything that has breath praise the Lord **(Ps 150:1-2,6).** O Lord, my Lord how excellent is Your name in all the earth **(Ps 8:1)**! The name of the Lord is a strong tower and the righteous run into it and are safe **(Prov 18:10).** O magnify the Lord with me, and let's exalt His name together **(Ps 34:3).** The Lord's name is to be praised from the rising of the sun to the going down of the same **(Ps 113:3).** Every day I will bless You Lord, and I will praise Your name forever and ever **(Ps 145:2).**

(Continue to bless the Lord and give thanks for
all that He has done for you.)

The Brazen Altar

Thy Kingdom Come

Ex 27:1-3

And thou shalt make an altar of shittim wood, five cubits long, and five cubits broad; the altar shall be foursquare: and the height thereof shall be three cubits. And thou shalt make the horns of it upon the four corners thereof: his horns shall be of the same: and thou shalt overlay it with brass. And thou shalt make his pans to receive his ashes, and his shovels, and his basons, and his fleshhooks, and his firepans: all the vessels thereof thou shalt make of brass.

The Brazen Altar

Lev 17:11
For the life of the flesh is in the blood: and I have given it to you upon the altar to make an atonement for your souls: for it is the blood that maketh an atonement for the soul.

The Brazen Altar of Sacrifice was where the animals were sacrificed to make atonement for sins of the Israelites. God ordained that the blood of innocent animals would cover or atone for the sins of human beings. Calvary was the Lord's Brazen Altar where the Lamb of God became our "Eternal Sacrifice".

Jesus Our Mighty Conquering Hero

Col 2:14-15
Blotting out the handwriting of ordinances that was against us, which was contrary to us, and took it out of the way, nailing it to his cross; And having spoiled principalities and powers, he made a shew of them openly, triumphing over them in it.

The word *"blotting"* means to smear out, obliterate, erase tears, and pardon sin. It also means removing, loosing, and putting away sin. The *"handwriting of ordinances"* was a legal document pronouncing us guilty and worthy of death. Verse 14 states that Jesus *"took it out of the way"* and erased the guilty verdict by nailing it to His cross! Verse 15 states, that *"he spoiled principalities and powers and made a shew of them openly"*!

The Greek definitions reflect a picture of a conquering hero who strips his defeated foe of all of his weapons. While he is standing naked of power, he is led off as a captive and paraded openly in total humiliation. This is what Jesus did to satan and his demons! Psalms 24 gives us the picture of the victory celebration in heaven. Our Lord is hailed and exalted as the Lord strong and mighty and the Lord mighty in battle returning with the spoils of this victory! God the Father exalted Jesus and gave Him the keys of hell and of death according to Revelation 1:18. He also gave Him a position *"far above all principality, and power, and might, and dominion, and every name that is named, not only in this world, but also in that which is to come: And hath put all things under his feet and gave him to be the head over all things to the church"* (Ephesians 1:21-22). Praise His Wonderful Name!

The Priests Were Anointed With Blood

The blood of the sacrifice was the foundation of the Tabernacle of Moses and the only foundation for worship and fellowship with God. Likewise, Christianity is based upon the foundation of the Blood of Jesus Christ. In the Tabernacle the blood was sprinkled upon everything, including the priests.

Lev 8:23-24
And he slew it; and Moses took of the blood of it, and put it upon the tip of Aaron's right ear, and upon the thumb of his right hand, and upon the great toe of his right foot. And he brought Aaron's sons, and Moses put of the blood upon the tip of their right ear, and upon the thumbs of their right hands, and upon the great toes of their right feet: and Moses sprinkled the blood upon the altar round about.

We can ask the Lord to anoint us so that we can minister unto Him. When we pray, we ask God to anoint our right ear with the Blood of Jesus, so we can hear what the Spirit is saying unto us. We ask Him to anoint our right thumb for *"our hands to war and our fingers to fight"*. We also ask Him to anoint our right toe, so we can walk in His ways and receive the anointing to crush the enemy under our feet.

As king-priests, we should recognize the power of the Blood of Jesus in every realm. The blood of the sacrifice was sprinkled upon everything in the Tabernacle, from the front gate to the Holy of Holies. This is perfect shadow picture of following the "pathway" made by the blood as you enter the gates. Our prayer in the Pattern of the Tabernacle is based upon the foundation of the Lamb of God shedding His Blood for us, making a way to enter our Father's presence!

The Blood Has A Voice

Gen 4:10
And he said, What hast thou done? the voice of thy brother's blood crieth unto me from the ground.

Heb 12:24
And to Jesus the mediator of the new covenant, and to the blood of the sprinkling, that speaketh better things than that of Abel.

Shattering Our Theology

A friend of ours shattered our theology one day when she said; we do not understand what was happening in the Garden of Gethsemane. She went on to say that Jesus was not shrinking from the thoughts of His impending death. She declared that in the Garden of Gethsemane, Jesus was actually trying to pass the Blood from His body! We were so shocked, yet we found ourselves meditating upon that thought.

Matt 26:38-39
Then saith he unto them, My soul is exceeding sorrowful, even unto death: tarry ye here, and watch with me. And he went a little farther, and fell on his face, and prayed, saying, O my Father, if it be possible, LET THIS CUP PASS FROM ME: nevertheless not as I will, but as thou wilt.

At the Last Supper Jesus clearly states that this cup is for the remission of sins!

Matt 26:26-28
And as they were eating, Jesus took bread, and blessed it, and break it, and gave it to the disciples, and said, Take, eat; this is my body.

And he took THE CUP, and gave thanks, and gave it to them, saying, Drink ye all of it; For this is my blood of the new testament which is shed for many for the remission of sins.

During the Passover meal, four cups of wine were consumed. The first cup was called the ***"Cup of Sanctification"*** because it consecrated the whole meal. The second cup was called the ***"Cup of Praise"***. The third cup was called the ***"Cup of Blessing"*** or ***"Cup of Redemption"*** which represented the blood of the Passover Lamb. The fourth cup was called the ***"Cup of Elijah"***. It was the third cup Jesus was speaking of in Matthew 26:27-28 when He declared this cup called the ***"Cup of Blessing"*** was His Blood that was shed for our sins. In I Corinthians 10:16 the Apostle Paul confirmed that the Blood of Jesus is the ***"Cup of Blessing"***.

I Cor 10:16
The CUP OF BLESSING which we bless, is it not the communion of the blood of Christ? The bread which we break, is it not the communion of the body of Christ?

We began to question why Jesus, the Lamb slain before the foundation of the world, born for the purpose of dying, would seemingly not want to die! Why would He rebuke Peter so strongly for trying to prevent His death, and then pray to escape it Himself?

We have been taught Jesus was sorrowful regarding the separation from God the Father that He knew He would experience when He allowed Himself to be made sin for us. While this is true, we have misunderstood what Jesus was really trying to accomplish in the Garden of Gethsemane. He was trying to pass the Blood, which was the ***"cup of blessing"***, from His body to redeem mankind! When Jesus prayed that the cup pass FROM Him, He was actually asking for this cup to pass OUT of Him and not AWAY from Him. The Greek word ***"pass"*** means basically ***"out of"*** and not ***"away from"***.

Isa 53:10-11
Yet it pleased the LORD to BRUISE him; he hath put him to grief: when thou shalt make his soul an offering for sin, he shall see his seed, he shall prolong his days, and the pleasure of the LORD shall prosper in

*his hand. **HE SHALL SEE OF THE TRAVAIL OF HIS SOUL, AND SHALL BE SATISFIED: by his knowledge shall my righteous servant justify many; for he shall bear their iniquities.***

We know Jesus knew all things concerning His days upon the earth. He also knew the exact timing of these things. While in the Garden of Gethsemane, Jesus knew Judas had betrayed Him and the Jewish leaders would have him arrested shortly. Knowing His time was limited, Jesus prayed for this cup to pass OUT of Him. The only way that this could be accomplished was for the Father to **BRUISE** Him. The word *"bruise"* means to crush, break, and cause injury without breaking the skin. Ruptured blood vessels and discoloration often characterize this. Bruise also means to hurt, especially psychologically. This bruising caused internal bleeding, therefore causing great drops of Blood to pass from His body.

We have heard doctors say, when a person bleeds from their pores, they are close to death. Can you imagine the delicate balance that had to be achieved, so He could remain alive and still endure the crucifixion? *God the Father had to place the iniquity of all mankind, past, present, and future, upon the sinless Lamb of God. Jesus was not reluctant but more than ready to complete all that was written about Him!* In Matthew 26:38, Jesus asked the disciples to pray with Him. It was during this time that He was waiting on the hand of the Father to bruise Him.

Luke 22:43-44
*And there appeared an angel unto him from heaven, **STRENGTHENING HIM. And being in an agony he prayed more earnestly: and his sweat was as it were GREAT DROPS OF BLOOD FALLING DOWN TO THE GROUND.***

We find in verse 43, an angel strengthened Jesus prior to His sweating great drops of Blood. Please note He was strengthened first; THEN He released the Blood! The angel was sent to strengthen Him so that He could release His Blood, the *"cup of blessing"*!

Have you wondered why the disciples went to sleep? Their spirits could not handle what was taking place. They fell asleep because the atmosphere was filled with all the iniquities of mankind as they were being poured into the sinless soul of Jesus. In the Garden of Gethsemane Jesus was yielding Himself to the hand of the Father to bruise Him with our iniquities so He could accomplish the TRAVAIL OF HIS SOUL. According to Isaiah 53:11, the Father would see the fruit of this travail and be satisfied.

The Blood Breaks The Curse

When God judged the sin of Adam, He pronounced a curse upon the ground (Genesis 3:17). In order for Jesus to redeem mankind, He had to start with the dust of the earth, the essence of which man was made. According to Genesis 4:10 and Hebrews 12:24, there is a special property about blood that enables it to speak. Because the Blood of Jesus speaks better things than that of Abel, the Blood Jesus released in Gethsemane was speaking forth and prophesying the redemption of all mankind. The Blood of the last Adam cried for mercy, love, restoration, and reconciliation. The Lord Jesus Christ was redeeming in the Garden of Gethsemane what the first Adam lost in the Garden of Eden. The first Adam lost the Glory of God, fellowship, and the ability to be fruitful—to shine with the glory and power of God. Jesus came to break the curse that was upon us so all these things could be restored.

The first reference to the blood speaking or having a voice can be found in Genesis 4:10. God was speaking to Cain about the murder of his brother Abel; *"And he said, What hast thou done? The voice of thy brother's blood crieth unto me from the ground".* Verse 11 states, that now Cain was cursed FROM the earth, which had received his brother's blood at his hand. The innocent blood of Abel spoke and cursed his brother from the earth. Throughout history there has been much innocent blood that has been shed. Can you imagine the curse this blood has been speaking against mankind? The Blood of Jesus that spoke from the earth in Gethsemane broke the curse the earth was speaking against guilty mankind.

Genesis 4:12 states, *"when thou tillest the ground, it shall not henceforth yield unto thee her strength; a fugitive and a vagabond shalt thou be in the earth".*

The curse "FROM" the earth against Cain, was the voice of innocent blood, producing a VAGABOND spirit. The word *"vagabond"* means drifting, aimless, wandering, unsettled, unfixed, purposeless, futile, and pointless. There is indication in scripture that Abel offered the required blood sacrifice unto the Lord and Cain brought fruits and vegetables, his effort of the flesh (Genesis 4:3-5). He did not bring the blood, which is the ONLY FOUNDATION FOR WORSHIP! Instead he became jealous and killed Abel because his blood offering was acceptable worship unto the Lord. Cain's life became a LIVING DEATH, with no aim, no purpose, and no clue because he did not understand the value of the blood! Doesn't that describe a major portion of humanity?

If we do not have a revelation of the power or the importance of the Blood of Jesus, we cannot bring acceptable sacrifices of praise. Therefore, we do not have the life of God and His power in our prayers! Our lives will not line up with the true plan and purpose of God, and cannot yield the maximum harvest. The Blood of Jesus broke that vagabond curse over us, so we could know our TRUE DESTINY and PURPOSE and find REST in Him!

In Leviticus 17:11, we are told that the life of the flesh is in the blood, and God has given it to us upon the altar to make atonement for our souls. It is only the *"Life of God"* that is in the Blood of Jesus that can produce life out of death and break the curse of sin and death. The Blood of Jesus is the only substance in the universe that could restore everything in every realm, and answer every charge that sin could possibly bring against mankind. THE BLOOD OF JESUS IS AWESOME!

On the Day of Atonement, the blood of the sacrifice was applied to the Mercy Seat and seven times before it on the ground (Leviticus 16:14). The blood applied seven times on the ground was prophetic of the Blood of Jesus possessing the sum total of perfection to completely redeem the earth and we who were made from the earth! It was foreshadowing what our Lord accomplished in Gethsemane when He sweat great drops of Blood. The Incarnation enabled Jesus to bring the Blood of God to the earth. He carried it for thirty years and released it at the appointed time! Hallelujah, Praise His Wonderful Matchless Name!

When we reflect upon the agonies that our Lord went through in the Garden of Gethsemane, it evokes the highest praise from within us. Each day in the Tabernacle Prayer, we extol our conquering hero at the Brazen Altar, which is symbolic of Gethsemane and Calvary. As king-priests, filled with revelation knowledge, we have the power to activate the awesome benefits of the Blood of Jesus. We declare that His Blood has a voice, and this voice speaks redemption, restoration and deliverance!

The Voice Of The Blood

When Adam sinned, God felt that separation, and He called to Adam *"where art thou?"* The voice of God calls out from the Blood of Jesus in earnest longings to a lost and dying world, *"where art thou?"* The Blood is speaking redemption to the unsaved; while at the same time it is calling out to His children to enter into God's presence as king-priests. Revelation 5:9-10 declares that Jesus redeemed us by His Blood, and made us kings and priests unto our God to rule and reign on this earth.

In summary, God came out of His throne room, stepping out of eternity into time, to be born as a man. He proceeded to fulfill the Law of God by living a sinless life. He accomplished the travail of His soul in the *"Garden of Gethsemane"* and continued to the *"Brazen Altar of Calvary"* to be our *"Holy Sin Offering"*. He then became the *"Scapegoat"* for our sins and took them to hell. After three days He arose victorious over death, hell, and the grave. In Revelation 1:18, Jesus declares that He lives and was dead, and is alive for evermore; and has the keys of hell and death. Hallelujah! He is the Lord of Hosts, the Lord strong and mighty, and the King of Glory, victorious over all of His enemies!

Thy Kingdom Come
(Matt 6:10)

When we thank God for the Blood of Jesus, we are praising Him that His Kingdom has come to earth, by way of the Lord Jesus Christ. He came to establish the Kingdom of God on earth, which is His rule, reign, dominion and order of doing things. Adam's original mandate was to subdue the earth, through God's power and dominion. Jesus came as the last Adam, to restore us to that original state. The Kingdom of God can only be established on this earth, as we recognize the power and authority of the Blood of Jesus in our daily lives.

Model For Creating
Your Own Prayer

2. Thank God For The Blood Of Jesus Christ
FATHER, THANK YOU FOR THE BLOOD OF JESUS CHRIST.
[Thy Kingdom Come]

The Prayer Pattern

Prayer:

2. The Brazen Altar

FATHER, THANK YOU FOR THE BLOOD OF JESUS CHRIST.
[Thy Kingdom Come]

Father, thank You for loving me so much that You gave Your only begotten Son, that whosoever shall believe in Him should not perish but have everlasting life (John 3:16). He was wounded for my transgressions, He was bruised for my iniquities: the chastisement of my peace was upon Him; and with His stripes I am healed (Isa 53:5). Thank You Lord Jesus for blotting out the handwriting of the ordinances that were against me and taking them out of the way by nailing them to Your cross. In the process You defeated and triumphed over every evil power and made a show of them openly (Col 2:14-15). Father God, I thank You for the precious Blood of Jesus that was shed for the remission of all my sins. I plead and apply the Blood of Jesus to every part of my life and upon every precious stone in my breastplate. **Gal 3:13** assures me that Christ has redeemed me from every curse over my life, that I may partake of the blessings of Abraham. Thank You Lord Jesus for redeeming me by Your Blood and making me a king-priest unto God to reign on this earth **(Rev 5:9-10).** Father I thank You that Your kingdom has come in my life.

The Brazen Laver

Thy Will Be Done

Ex 30:18-21

Thou shalt also make a laver of brass, and his foot also of brass, to wash withal: and thou shalt put it between the tabernacle of the congregation and the altar, and thou shalt put water therein. For Aaron and his sons shall wash their hands and their feet thereat: When they go into the tabernacle of the congregation, they shall wash with water, that they die not; or when they come near to the altar to minister, to burn offering made by fire unto the LORD: So they shall wash their hands and their feet, that they die not: and it shall be a statute for ever to them, even to him and to his seed throughout their generations.

The Brazen Laver

The second piece of furniture in the Outer Court was the Brazen Laver and it was filled with water. The priests would wash their hands and feet at this Laver before performing their priestly duties. The first time Aaron and His sons were washed, the washing was done for them by another (Moses), as stated in Exodus 29:4. This is a type of our new birth where the Lord washed and redeemed us from the original sin of Adam. The water also symbolized the cleansing power of the Word of God. Notice that after the initial washing, it was then the responsibility of the priests to wash themselves before performing ANY PRIESTLY DUTIES in the Tabernacle. They were to wash their hands and feet, their WORKS and their WALK.

Before we minister unto the Lord in prayer, we should wash ourselves with the Word of repentance. Ephesians 5:26-27 states: *"That he might sanctify and cleanse it with the washing of water by the word, That he might present it to himself a glorious church, not having spot, or wrinkle, or any such thing; but that it should be holy and without blemish"*.

In John 13:5, we see a demonstration of the Lord Jesus performing this washing when He washed the feet of His disciples. They were washed with the water by the Word! The Lord also prayed in John 17:17, that we would be sanctified or *"set apart"* by the truth of the Word of God. As the Word separates us from the world unto God, we can then find our unique place in the plans and purposes of God. We cannot go forward into our king-priest calling without being washed with the water by the Word.

The Word Of God Is God

John 1:1
In the beginning was the Word, and the Word was with God, and the Word was God....

The Word of God is God. When you pray, declare and decree the Word of God you are sending forth God Himself!

Rev 19:11-13
And I saw heaven opened, and behold a white horse; and he that sat upon him was called Faithful and True, and in righteousness he doth judge and make war. His eyes were as a flame of fire, and on his head were many crowns; and he had a name written, that no man knew, but he himself. And he was clothed with a vesture dipped in blood: and his name is called The Word of God.

The Word of God is Jesus and we need to change our thinking about how powerful the Word of God truly is!

John 1:2-3
The same was in the beginning with God. All things were made by him; and without him was not any thing made that was made.

Absolutely nothing in heaven or earth was made without the Word of God. We can clearly see this truth in Genesis Chapter one as God spoke the Word and all things were created. We, being made in His likeness and image, also must speak the Word of God so it can be established in our lives and upon this earth.

One of the main reasons that God has called all men to a king-priest ministry is the fact that nothing is established on this earth unless it is spoken first.

Heb 4:12
For the word of God is quick, and powerful, and sharper than any twoedged sword, piercing even to the dividing asunder of soul and spirit, and of the joints and marrow, and is a discerner of the thoughts and intents of the heart.

The Word of God is the most powerful living force in the universe. According to Psalms 138:2, God exalts His Word above His name. Adam was led by his spirit before he fell into sin. When he decided to follow his emotions instead of the Word of God, his soul and spirit became intermingled. He was no longer spirit-led as God had designed him. He became a being, led by his five senses. The SOUL is the emotions, will, thoughts, and intellect and the SPIRIT is the part of our being that communicates with God. The only force that can divide the soul from the spirit is the living Word of God. Division is necessary so we can walk in the wisdom of God. As king-priests unto God, we are to declare and decree His Word, not our opinions or circumstances, because His Word is all-powerful.

The Cleansing Power Of The Word

Eph 5:26-27
That he might SANCTIFY and CLEANSE it with the WASHING of WATER by the WORD, That he might present it to himself a glorious church, not having spot, or wrinkle, or any such thing; but that it should be holy and without blemish.

The word *"sanctify"*, means to make holy, purify or consecrate. It also means to make physically pure or morally blameless. The word *"cleanse"* means to make clean, purge and purify. The Word of God will not only clean, but it will purge you by getting rid of the junk that lies deep within. The word *"washing"* means a bath. It also means to cleanse the face, hands, feet and garments. The Word of God will bathe you so that you can face all things without guilt. It will bathe your hands and feet so that your works and your walk will be clean. It will also wash your garments so you can become a priest unto God and intercede for others. The word *"water"* means to rain as in a shower. The Word of God is a rain shower – a shower of power! The Word of God has the power to cleanse, purify and sanctify. The only way to be transformed into the glorious Church is BY THE WASHING OF WATER BY THE WORD!

We Build Our Faith By The Word of God

The Word tells us that without faith it is impossible to please God (Hebrews 11:6). Romans 10:17 tells us that faith comes by hearing and hearing by the Word of God. This double reference to hearing tells us that we must continue to hear the Word of God in order to build faith. It also tells us that faith, the assurance and belief in the Word, comes by two different types of "hearing". As defined in the Greek, the first is receptive; the act of hearing, being part of the audience. The second type is active; to give or to report.

With this Prayer Pattern, you will be performing both kinds of hearing at the same time. You will be speaking the Word and hearing the Word simultaneously, thereby building faith! As you do this daily, you will experience a new level of faith and intimacy with God that you never knew was possible. You will come to understand the scriptures more clearly as God pours out revelation upon you concerning His Word. You will also experience a greater anointing, a deeper fellowship, and true communion with the Father. Never again will you experience a dry, unproductive prayer time. You will be in the presence of the Lord – the Secret Place of the Most High!

Be A Doer Of The Word

According to Exodus 38:8, the Laver had mirrors in it. James 1:22-25, tells us that the Word of God must be applied to our lives. We must look into the Laver of God's Word, as we would a mirror, and wash ourselves with it. We are to look into the Word, see our condition versus what God says about us, and make a decision to walk in His truth. We are not to forget what we see, what we hear, or what *"manner of man"* we are. But we are to continue in the perfect law of liberty. There are two laws at work on this earth. We, as Christians, can choose which law we will live under. According to Romans 8:2, there is the *"law of sin and death"*, and there is the *"law of the Spirit of life in Christ Jesus"*. Whichever law we choose to live under will determine our effectiveness in this life. In order to live under the *"law of the spirit of life in Christ Jesus"*, we must say what the Word of God says about us. We must declare Who He is, and who we are in Him.

Remember the Tabernacle of Moses is also called the *"Tabernacle of Testimony"*. We overcome by the Blood of the Lamb and the word of our testimony. Our testimony of the life, death, resurrection, and glorification of the Lord Jesus Christ will lead us to victory! We operate in our calling as king-priests when we declare the Word of God. According to Hebrews 3:1, Jesus is the Apostle and High Priest of our profession or confession. Therefore, He is anointed to bring every word to pass that we speak, WHEN we speak His Word!

Thy Will Be Done
(Matt 6:10)

The Word of God is the will of God. Therefore when we pray the Word, we are declaring: "Thy will be done". Psalms 119:89 states, "For ever, O LORD, thy word is settled in heaven". The Word of God is settled in heaven, and the only way to settle or establish it on earth is for us to pray or speak it.

Model For Creating
Your Own Prayer

3. Thank God For His Word
[Thy Will Be Done]

_____
_____
_____
_____
_____
_____
_____
_____
_____
_____
_____
_____
_____
_____
_____
_____
_____
_____

The Prayer Pattern

Prayer:

3.   The Brazen Laver
FATHER THANK YOU FOR YOUR WORD.
[Thy Will Be Done]

Father, I thank You that **John 1:1** says, in the beginning was the Word, and the Word was with God, and the Word was God. **John 1:14** says that the Word was made flesh, and dwelt among us, (and we beheld His Glory, the glory of the only begotten of the Father), full of grace and truth. Jesus is the Word made flesh. Your Word is made flesh or manifested in my life, as I establish Your Word upon this earth. Your Word is health and healing to all of my flesh **(Prov 4:22)**. Your Word is quick and powerful and sharper than any two-edged sword and is able to divide the soul and spirit, the joints and marrow, and discern the thoughts and intents of the heart **(Heb 4:12)**. Your Word is a lamp unto my feet, and a light unto my path **(Ps 119:105)**. I receive the blessings of **Deut 28:1-14**, because I hearken diligently unto Your Word. I thank You Father that I have been sanctified and cleansed with the washing of water by the Word of God **(Eph 5:26)**. Your Word is Your will; therefore let Your will be done in my life.

The Gate Called "Truth"

Ex 26:36-37

*And thou shalt make an hanging for the door of the tent, of blue,
and purple, and scarlet, and fine twined linen, wrought with
needlework. And thou shalt make for the hanging five
pillars of shittim wood, and overlay them with gold,
and their hooks shall be of gold: and thou shalt
cast five sockets of brass for them.*

Chapter 8

The Gate Called "Truth"

Gate Called "The Truth"

The Gate called "The Truth" is the entrance to the Holy Place or Inner Court. The five pillars in the Gate represent "grace" and the five-fold ministry gifts. Only the priesthood could go beyond this point. Everything in the Tabernacle was built and functioned for the worship and reverence of God. There was no room for the priests to do their own thing or fulfill their own desires! Today many are building their own kingdoms instead of the Kingdom of God. We could all learn something about how this priesthood operated!

As New Testament king-priests, we enter this Gate, and begin to understand the higher purposes of God and His heart for lost souls! We are no longer praying selfish prayers like the old farmer when he said: *"God bless me and my wife, my son John and his wife; us four no more!"*

We have to constantly ask ourselves; *"What was Calvary for --- if not for the souls?"* Jesus died a painful and horrible death to redeem mankind, and our purpose and destiny is to pray and intercede for them to receive their redemption. We should want to ensure that Jesus receives His full reward; every soul He suffered, bled and died for! Everything we do in life should be to further that end and to be in harmony with the heart of God.

The bottom line is that you really have to want to know the truth to enter beyond this Gate. You have to want to know the heart of God and how much He loves the souls of mankind. Most Christians spend their entire life in the Outer Court and never move beyond that point in their relationship with the Lord. That is why many do not have a burden for lost souls. As we continue beyond this Gate of Truth, we will be closer to having the Lord's love perfected in us and His heart for lost souls.

We were born to the kingdom for such a time as this; to receive our king-priest ministry and continue the journey into His presence and His Glory. And we are destined to manifest His Glory upon this earth and bring in the Lord's end-time harvest of souls!

Leaving the Outer Court, and going past this Gate, the priests would enter into the Holy Place. The Holy Place is where the Candlestick, the Table of Shewbread and the Altar of Incense were housed. The Holy Place was only for the priests. In order to enter in, you had to be "born" into the priesthood. It is the same today; you cannot enter into the Holy Place unless you have been "born-again" and have a desire to fulfill your calling to the priesthood.

The Golden Candlestick

In Earth, As It Is In Heaven

Ex 25:31-32

And thou shalt make a candlestick of pure gold: of beaten work shall the candlestick be made: his shaft, and his branches, his bowls, his knops, and his flowers, shall be of the same. And six branches shall come out of the sides of it; three branches of the candlestick out of the one side, and three branches of the candlestick out of the other side:

The Golden Candlestick

The Golden Candlestick

The Golden Candlestick is the third piece of furniture that we encounter on our journey. The Candlestick was made of pure gold, consisting of a center branch, and six other branches proceeding from the center branch. Each branch had a lamp containing pure olive oil, and was to be kept burning continually. It was the only light in the Holy Place and illuminated everything. Jesus said in John 8:12; *"I am the light of the world: he that followeth me shall not walk in darkness, but shall have the light of life"*. The "light of life" that is promised to those who follow Him is the "Glory of God!" In Matthew 5:14-16, Jesus declares that we are the light of the world and partakers of the Glory of God. The light or glory will be so evident, that those in darkness will see our good works and glorify our Heavenly Father!

We should remember it was the continual supply of oil that brought forth the light (Exodus 27:20). We must spend time in God's presence daily to receive our fresh refilling or supply of oil. We should ask the Lord for His correction, or trimming of our wicks. We want to be that Candlestick, burning brightly and reflecting divine light. Also according to Exodus 25:31, the Candlestick, like our Savior, was hammered and beaten. But notice that the hammering yielded beautiful resurrection life in the form of buds, blossoms, and fruit.

The Lord Jesus Christ was beaten and crucified that we might experience "new" life in Him. There were seven branches in the Candlestick denoting the perfection of the sevenfold anointing as described in Isaiah 11:2. The Lord Jesus Christ embodied the sevenfold Spirit of God and according to Acts 10:38 and I John 3:8, Jesus was anointed with the Holy Ghost and power to heal the oppressed and to destroy the works of the devil. We are also anointed with the Holy Ghost and power, and will be that Lampstand burning brightly to duplicate Christ's ministry in the earth.

The Light Of The World

John 8:12
Then spake Jesus again unto them, saying, I am the light of the world: he that followeth me shall not walk in darkness, but shall have the light of life.

The *"light of life"* is the Glory of God, that we are destined to walk in. In Matthew 5:14, Jesus said we are the light of the world, and a city set upon a hill that cannot be hidden. There have been many prophetic words concerning believers, in these last days, walking in the glory and the power of God. Yet, false humility and unbelief have kept us from declaring it and praying for it to be manifested in our lives.

Rev 1:20
The mystery of the seven stars which thou sawest in my right hand, and the seven golden candlesticks. The seven stars are the angels of the seven churches: and the seven candlesticks which thou sawest are the seven churches.

Revelation 1:20, reveals that the Church of God is represented as seven golden candlesticks. In the Old Testament, the priest would enter into the Holy Place daily to dress the Candlestick. He would first trim the wicks, deposit fresh olive oil, and re-ignite it so it would burn brightly each day.

In prayer, we declare that we are the *"light of the world"*, the golden candlesticks or lampstands. We then ask the Lord Jesus Christ, our High Priest, to trim our wicks and cut away all things that are not pleasing to Him. We also ask for a fresh refilling of anointing oil and to be set on fire anew. This is the type of prayer that we should pray over the five-fold ministry, the entire Body of Christ, and ourselves. When there is no hindrance to the *"light"* of God flowing through us, the world will see our good works and glorify our Father in heaven. One of the greatest benefits of having the Glory of God manifested upon us is holy protection. God says in Isaiah 4:5, that there will be a *"DEFENSE"* upon the glory. As darkness quickly approaches, every Christian should be clothed in the glory and protection of God.

The Gospel Of The Kingdom

Matt 9:35
Then Jesus went about all the cities and villages, teaching in their synagogues, <u>PREACHING THE GOSPEL OF THE KINGDOM,</u> and healing every sickness and every disease among the people.

Matt 10:7-8
... And as you go, preach, saying,'The kingdom of heaven is at hand.' Heal the sick, cleanse the lepers, raise the dead, cast out demons.

Three elements are connected and we see them in these scriptures. They are the proclamation of the Gospel of the Kingdom, healing and casting out demons.

Luke 4:18-19

The Spirit of the Lord is upon me, because he hath anointed me to preach the gospel to the poor; he hath sent me to heal the brokenhearted, to preach deliverance to the captives, and recovering of sight to the blind, to set at liberty them that are bruised, To preach the acceptable year of the Lord.

This is how Jesus began His earthly ministry in His hometown, Nazareth.

Acts 10:38
How God anointed Jesus of Nazareth with the Holy Ghost and with power: who went about doing good, and healing all that were oppressed of the devil; for God was with him.

We need to proclaim these scriptures! And then declare; *"The good news is that I'm anointed with the same Holy Spirit and power and I go about doing good and healing all who are oppressed by devil, for God the Father is with me!"* The truth is that some things will never become a reality in our spirit unless we continually declare them over ourselves building that Word on the inside.

Acts 3:6
Then Peter said, Silver and gold have I none; but such as I have give I thee: In the name of Jesus Christ of Nazareth rise up and walk.

Peter had something! He had healing, in the name of Jesus Christ to give to him! The Gospel of the Kingdom is the good news that the Holy Spirit was upon Jesus to bring deliverance to every man. And we have received the same power of the Holy Spirit to proclaim the life, death, resurrection, glorification, and total dominion of Jesus Christ and to duplicate his ministry in the earth!

This reveals to us that the Tabernacle Prayer is very powerful, because when we declare it, we are in fact proclaiming the "Gospel of the Kingdom". We are declaring everything Jesus accomplished and who we are in Him!

Matt 24:14

And this gospel of the kingdom shall be preached in all the world for a witness unto all nations; and then shall the end come.

1 Cor 2:4

And my speech and my preaching was not with enticing words of man's wisdom, but in demonstration of the Spirit and of power:

In Earth, As It Is In Heaven
(Matt 6:10)

As we thank God for the anointing of the Holy Spirit, we activate His power in our lives. He is Almighty God, the Comforter and the Spirit of Truth, Who was sent to manifest the glory of heaven on this earth.

Model For Creating
Your Own Prayer

4. Thank God For The Anointing Of The Holy Spirit
FATHER THANK YOU FOR THE ANOINTING OF THE HOLY SPIRIT.
[In Earth, As It Is In Heaven]

The Prayer Pattern

Prayer:

4. The Golden Candlestick
FATHER THANK YOU FOR THE ANOINTING OF THE HOLY SPIRIT.
[In Earth, As It Is In Heaven]

In **John 8:12** Jesus said, I am the Light of the world and he that follows Me shall not walk in darkness but shall have the light of life. Father thank You for the *"light of life"*, which is the anointing. Jesus is the "Light of the world" and He has caused me to be a reflector of that light which will bring glory to my Heavenly Father **(Matt 5:14-16). Acts 10:38** states, that God anointed Jesus of Nazareth with the Holy Ghost and with power: who went about doing good, and healing all that were oppressed of the devil; for God was with Him. I am also anointed with the Holy Spirit and I am born of God for the purpose of destroying the works of darkness **(I John 3:8).** Jesus said in **John 14:12,** he that believes on Me, the works that I do he shall do also, and greater works than these. Thank You Lord for the anointing and the gifts of the Holy Spirit to do these greater works. I ask You Holy Spirit to flow through me as You purpose with the gift of faith, gifts of healing, working of miracles, word of wisdom, word of knowledge, discerning of spirits, tongues, interpretation of tongues, and prophecy **(I Cor 12:8-10).** I have the sevenfold anointing; the spirit of the Lord, the spirit of wisdom and understanding, the spirit of counsel and might, the spirit of knowledge, and of the fear of the Lord **(Isa 11:2).** Father, correct me, so that nothing will hinder Your power from flowing through me and I can bring forth pure and holy light. Father, I thank You for the Holy Spirit, Who brings forth Your power from heaven. I also thank You for allowing me to share Your light all over this world.

The Table Of Shewbread

*Give Us This Day Our Daily Bread
And Forgive Us Our Debts, As We Forgive Our Debtors*

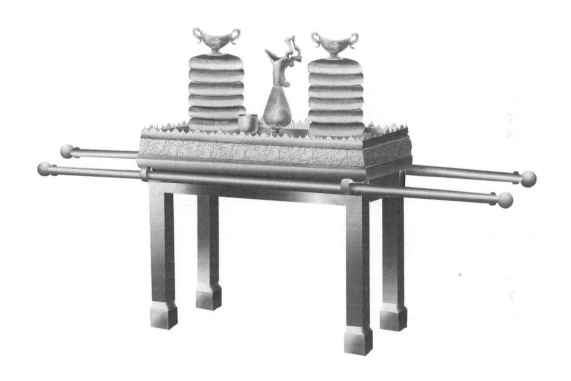

Ex 25:23-24,30

*Thou shalt also make a table of shittim wood: two cubits shall be the
length thereof, and a cubit the breadth thereof, and a cubit and a
half the height thereof. And thou shalt overlay it with pure gold,
and make thereto a crown of gold round about. And thou
shalt set upon the table shewbread before me alway.*

The Table Of Shewbread

The Shewbread

In the Old Testament this Table was for the priests of the Lord. Now it is the Table of the redeemed of the Lord, His royal priesthood (I Peter 2:9). There were twelve loaves of bread, symbolic of the twelve tribes of Israel only. But now they represent the entire world. The loaves of bread were perforated and sprinkled with frankincense. Every Sabbath the bread was replaced, and the former bread was given to the priests for food. When translating the word *"bread"*, it gives us the ability to war, battle, prevail, overcome, and be delivered. This Table also stood before the Lord, as a constant reminder of His love for His people. The words *"bread or shewbread"* also mean the *"presence bread"* or *"bread of faces"*. It was always in the Father's presence and continually before His face. The nation of Israel and the world are always on God's heart. We are loved and *"accepted in the beloved"*. We experience communion and sweet fellowship with God at this Table. The golden crown around the Table of Shewbread kept the bread from falling. This is a picture of Jude 24, which says that God is *"able to keep you from falling; and to present you faultless before the presence of His Glory with exceeding joy"*.

The Wine

The drink offering consisted of wine that was poured out as an offering unto the Lord. The priests were not to drink it according to Numbers 28:7. The wine was symbolic of the *"cup of blessing"* that the Lord Jesus poured out in the Garden of Gethsemane. The priests were not allowed to drink the wine, which was symbolic of the Lord's Blood, BECAUSE HE HAD NOT YET COME. But as New Testament king-priests, we are told by Jesus to eat His flesh and drink His Blood (Matthew 26:26-28). This is the communion of the Lord's Table.

The Father's Heart

The Table of Shewbread had four corners, representing the four corners of the earth. God's entire reason for the plan of redemption was to bring His family home! It bears repeating, that the Father's eyes always rested on this Table. Therefore, we must understand the importance of the great commission (Mark 16:15). We should always be mindful to pray that God will raise up laborers to reap His harvest of children.

(Step 1) - Repentance For All

The first thing we do at the Table of Shewbread is stand in the gap and repent for the unsaved, world leadership, the Body of Christ and the nation of Israel (Ezekiel 22:30). The names of the twelve tribes of Israel were inscribed on stones, which were worn on the shoulders of the High priest. He also had the stones representing the twelve tribes on his breastplate. In the spirit realm, we wear a breastplate also. Now these names and stones represent physical Israel, the Body of Christ, the unsaved, and world leadership. We, as king-priests of the Lord, are to pray that the world will be reconciled to Him.

We intercede or stand in the gap for them according to Ezekiel 22:30 and repent for them according to Daniel 9, Ezra 9, and II Chronicles 7:14. In our king-priest calling, it is powerful when we follow the examples of Daniel, Ezra, and Solomon, and repent for our fellowman. God wants to bring blessing, not judgment. But how can He bless those that are wayward, in rebellion, and living in sin? The answer is that He cannot. But we, as king-priests of the Lord, can stand in the gap and repent for them and declare the Word of God over their lives. When this is done, the Holy Spirit will work with them to bring them to a personal repentance and knowledge of the Lord.

Daniel 9:5 shows Daniel, as the perfect intercessor, identifying with the sins of his nation and asking for mercy and forgiveness. We, as born-again believers, have the ministry of reconciliation and the word of reconciliation according to II Corinthians 5:18-19. We are to use this ministry to reconcile ALL MEN unto God. Please note that the Table of Shewbread wording is PLURAL even if we are praying as an individual. It is at this point in the

Pattern that we become intercessors that identify with the sins of the world and repent for them.

Daniel's Prayer Of Repentance

Dan 9:5
WE HAVE SINNED, AND HAVE COMMITTED INIQUITY, AND HAVE DONE WICKEDLY, *and have rebelled, even by departing from thy precepts and from thy judgments:*

Dan 9:19
O LORD, HEAR; O LORD, FORGIVE; *O Lord, hearken and do; defer not, for thine own sake, O my God: for thy city and thy people are called by thy name.*

(Step 2) - Spiritually Partake Of Communion

This Table also represents the Lord as the *"Bread of Life"* (John 6:48). Therefore in prayer, we spiritually partake of the Bread and Wine, which brings life to every form of death in our lives. This *"Bread and Wine"* which God provided, gives us the ability to destroy our enemies and bring deliverance to all men. After spiritually partaking of the broken body and shed Blood of our Lord Jesus Christ, we understand that we have a Blood-bought covenant right to intercede and to be heard!

(Step 3) - Put On The Whole Armor Of God

We must be equipped and prepared to do battle for the people that God has placed on our hearts and shoulders. We are to put on the whole armor of God according to Ephesians 6:10-18. Whether we know it or not, when we open our mouths to do warfare, we are on the battlefield. It is spiritual suicide to enter the battlefield without the armor of God!

(Step 4) – Spiritual Warfare

We bind and break the power of the strong man and demonic forces, then loose the angels with the Word of God for our situation. It is important to bind the strong man because he is the ruler over the demonic stronghold. When we bind him, then we are able to destroy his power (Matthew 12:29). A major part of our covenant blessings involve the ministry of angels. The first chapter of Hebrews tells us that they are ministering spirits FOR THE HEIRS OF SALVATION. We have awesome power at our disposal, but we must speak the Word. The angels do not hearken to our opinions or our own words; they heed only the voice of God's Word. This means we must speak the Word of God, giving voice to it over every situation so the angels will have the necessary power to bring the victory (Psalms 103:20). We also need to pray with our Bibles open so the Lord can quicken different scriptures to us that need to be sown into the earth realm.

(Step 5) - Pray For The Unsaved, World Leadership, Body Of Christ, And Israel

We can now pray for and declare over every precious stone in our breastplates, the unsaved, leadership, Body of Christ and Israel. Constant prayer to the Lord of the Harvest should be made for the unsaved (Matthew 9:37-38). We are also told to make intercession for those in authority so that they may be saved and the gospel will have free course in the earth (I Timothy 2:1-4). And we, the Body of Christ, are encouraged to pray one for another (James 5:16-17).

The prayers of the Apostle Paul in Ephesians 1:17-23 and 3:14-21 are perfect prayers to bring about the glorification and perfection of the Church. Not only do they include wisdom and revelation for us to know the hope of His calling, but they also declare we have the resurrection power of Christ within us. These prayers also bring us to the point of knowing and understanding the love of God, so we can be filled with all the fullness of Christ.

Eph 1:17-23
That the God of our Lord Jesus Christ, the Father of glory, may give unto you the spirit of wisdom and revelation in the knowledge of him: The eyes of your understanding being enlightened; that ye may know what is the hope of his calling, and what the riches of the glory of his inheritance in the Saints, And what is the exceeding greatness of his

power to usward who believe, according to the working of his mighty power, Which he wrought in Christ, when he raised him from the dead, and set him at his own right hand in the heavenly places, Far above all principality, and power, and might, and dominion, and every name that is named, not only in this world, but also in that which is to come: And hath put all things under his feet, and gave him to be the head over all things to the church, Which is his body, the fulness of him that filleth all in all.

Eph 3:14-21
For this cause I bow my knees unto the Father of our Lord Jesus Christ, Of whom the whole family in heaven and earth is named, That he would grant you, according to the riches of His Glory, to be strengthened with might by his Spirit in the inner man; That Christ may dwell in your hearts by faith; that ye, being rooted and grounded in love, may be able to comprehend with all the Saints what is the width and length and depth and height—to know the love of Christ which passes knowledge; that you may be filled with all the fullness of God. Now unto him that is able to do exceeding abundantly above all that we ask or think, according to the power that worketh in us, Unto him be glory in the church by Christ Jesus throughout all ages, world without end. Amen.

Concerning Israel, we should delight in praying for the peace of Jerusalem because God's end-time plans and purposes will be fulfilled in the nation of Israel. In essence, when we pray for the peace of Jerusalem, we are praying for the return of the Lord Jesus Christ! In addition, we have been adopted by God and grafted into His Jewish family. Therefore, we have an obligation and the privilege to pray for our family members. God's Word states; *"Pray for the peace of Jerusalem; they shall prosper that love thee"* (Psalms 122:6). Psalms 122:9 says, *"because of the house of the LORD our God I will seek thy good"*. Many of us have never been taught to pray for Israel and bless them. God's promise to Abraham that a blessing would come upon those who would bless his seed still holds true (Genesis 12:3). When we truly understand the heart of God and our Jewish heritage, we will not fail to bless them daily.

Give Us This Day Our Daily Bread.
And Forgive Us Our Debts,
As We Forgive Our Debtors.
(Matt 6:11-12)

As king-priests, we stand in the gap and repent for all men. As we thank God for Jesus the "Bread of Life", we are thanking Him for His daily provision to do battle, overcome and be delivered. When we spiritually partake of communion and have fellowship with the Lord, we receive His full power. This prepares us to enter into spiritual warfare and intercede for all men.

Model For Creating
Your Own Prayer

5. Stand In The Gap, Repent, Intercede For The World

FATHER I STAND IN THE GAP AND REPENT FOR ALL. THANK YOU THAT JESUS IS THE BREAD OF LIFE AND MY POWER TO DO BATTLE. I SPIRITUALLY PARTAKE OF COMMUNION, PUT ON YOUR ARMOR AND INTERCEDE FIRST FOR YOUR PURPOSES AND THEN PRAY MY OWN PETITIONS.

[Give Us This Day Our Daily Bread. And Forgive Us Our Debts, As We Forgive Our Debtors]

_____

_____

_____

_____

_____

_____

_____

_____

_____

_____

_____
_____
_____
_____
_____
_____
_____
_____
_____
_____
_____
_____
_____
_____
_____

The Prayer Pattern

Prayer:

5. *The Table Of Shewbread*

FATHER I STAND IN THE GAP AND REPENT FOR ALL. THANK YOU THAT JESUS IS THE BREAD OF LIFE AND MY POWER TO DO BATTLE. I SPIRITUALLY PARTAKE OF COMMUNION, PUT ON YOUR ARMOR AND INTERCEDE FIRST FOR YOUR PURPOSES AND THEN PRAY MY OWN PETITIONS.
[Give Us This Day Our Daily Bread. And Forgive Us Our Debts, As We Forgive Our Debtors]

Father as I come to Your Table as a king-priest and intercessor, I stand in the gap for the Jews, the entire Body of Christ, the unsaved, and for the leaders of this world **(Ezek 22:30).** I stand in the gap and repent for we have all sinned, transgressed Your laws, committed iniquity, shed innocent blood, operated in unforgiveness, and have done wickedly in Your sight. **I John 1:9** says, if we confess our sins, You are faithful and just to forgive us. Father forgive and cleanse us with the Blood of Jesus. Father, as we spiritually partake of communion, the broken body and shed Blood of Jesus, we thank You that Jesus is the "Bread of Life". His body and Blood is our nourishment, strength and power to be victorious over all works of the enemy. It is also the "Children's Bread of Deliverance", therefore we are delivered from every foe within and without. We put on the whole armor of God according to **Eph 6:10-20.** We are strong in the Lord and in the power of His might. The weapons of our warfare are not carnal but they are mighty through God for the pulling down of strongholds **(II Cor 10: 4-5).** You have given us authority to tread upon serpents and scorpions, and over all of the power of the enemy and nothing shall by any means hurt us **(Luke 10:19).** We bind every strong man that is set against us and loose the Angel of the Lord to plunder their house and spoil their goods **(Matt 12:29).** According to **II Tim 4:18,** Father we declare that You will deliver us from every evil work and preserve us for Your heavenly kingdom. We pray that the unsaved will come to know Jesus Christ as Lord and Savior **(Ps 2:8).** We ask for the heathen nations as our inheritance and the uttermost parts of the earth as our possession. We also pray for the fear of God to fall upon every leader all over the world, thereby bringing them to repentance. We declare that Your people will lead a quiet and peaceable life in all godliness and honesty and the gospel of Jesus Christ will continue to spread unhindered all over the world **(I Tim 2:2).** Father we ask that we receive the spirit of wisdom and revelation in the knowledge of You, that the eyes of our understanding are enlightened that we might know the hope of our calling and to know the surpassing fullness of Your love **(Eph 1:17-23 - - 3:14-21).** We pray for the peace of Jerusalem, peace within their walls and prosperity within their palaces and we seek their highest good **(Ps 122:6-9).** Father, thank You for the blessing over our lives that You promised us for loving and praying for Israel **(Gen 12:3).** We pray that the Body of Christ will come into the unity of faith, unto the knowledge of the Son of God, unto a perfect man, to the measure of the stature of the fullness of Christ **(Eph 4:13).**

(You can now pray your own petitions)

Intercession And Communion

The Table of Shewbread

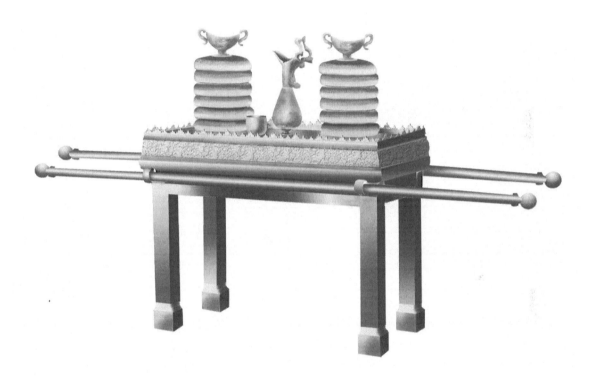

I Cor 11:26

**For as often as ye eat this bread, and drink this cup, ye
do show the Lord's death till he come.**

Intercession And Communion

Intercession

Praying according to Pattern will bring forth powerful intercession. The Tabernacle Prayer takes us through repentance. The Blood of Jesus and the water of His Word in the Outer Court cleanse us. As we go beyond the gate of TRUTH, we are illuminated and anointed at the Lampstand. We then prepare for warfare intercession at the Table of Shewbread. However, before warring for anyone---REPENT FOR THEM FIRST! We can use the examples that are in Daniel 9 and Ezra 9. These intercessors identified with and repented for the sins of their nation. Due to the fact that we are free agents, God will not force Himself upon us to love and accept Him. But when we, as king-priests stand in the gap and repent for others, God is faithful to go forth and begin to work in their lives. That is why God is always looking for a man to stand in the gap so judgment can be avoided (Ezekiel 22:30).

The next step we must do BEFORE warring is to put on the whole armor of God (Ephesians 6:10-20). Most people begin warfare without this process and they enter the spiritual battlefield unprotected. Entering the battlefield without our armor is spiritual suicide! We have noticed while ministering deliverance, there are people who have spiritual warfare wounds, due to going into battle against the enemy without the proper protection.

It is vitally important to our welfare to put on our armor before entering spiritual warfare. The fiery darts of the wicked one are not felt physically. They wound our spirit man thereby draining us of power and energy. Then slowly but surely it manifests in our soul man bringing about discouragement, hopelessness and other ungodly attitudes. This in turn leaves us open to attacks in our physical bodies. So please understand that we must put on our armor before we get on the battlefield.

Communion

The *"Bread"* represents the broken body of Jesus Christ, which is our nourishment and strength to do battle, to prevail, and overcome. The *"Wine"* represents the shed Blood of Jesus for the remission of our sins. The *"Bread and Wine"* contains the **"Life of God"** needed to defeat every form of darkness in our lives. This life that we are talking about is not life as in a *"breathing entity"*, but it is *"zoe"*; God's kind of life—victorious life! At the Table of Shewbread, we spiritually partake of communion for all men and receive this *"zoe"* life within us. Another powerful point to recognize is the fact that Jesus came as a man anointed by the Holy Spirit. He defeated all demonic forces as the Son of Man, not as the Son of God. The Holy Spirit also anoints us, and by receiving communion we gain that same power to overcome our enemies.

John 6:53,56
Then Jesus said unto them, Verily, verily, I say unto you, Except ye eat the flesh of the Son of man, and drink his blood, ye have no life in you. He that eateth my flesh, and drinketh my blood, dwelleth in me, and I in him.

We take communion so God will dwell in us and we will dwell in Him. When we do this, the *"Light and Life of God"* destroys all darkness in and around us and gives us the power and authority to annihilate our enemies.

I Cor 11:26
For as often as ye eat this bread, and drink this cup, ye do show the Lord's death till he come.

This scripture states that we are to declare and decree the Lord's death, resurrection, and glorification every time we receive communion. He said as often as we do this, (take communion); we are to declare His praises! Declaring the victory of the Son of Man and partaking of His flesh and Blood empowers us to become like Him—anointed to destroy the works of the enemy! Each day when we pray according to Pattern, we spiritually partake of communion at the Table of Shewbread and receive His power! At the end of the Prayer, we usually **"physically"** take communion.

Jacob

Jacob is a prophetic archetype of a mighty king-priest intercessor. You will see in the following pages that this type of intercessor produces the kind of repentance that God needs to forgive our sins and heal our land. The covenant confirmed in Jacob is our covenant of *"transformation and intercession"*. And this will bring about the desire of the Father's heart and His end-time purposes in the earth.

The House Of God

After Jacob received the birthright blessings from his father, Esau threatened to kill him. When Rebekah learned of the threats she advised Jacob to leave and go to her brother Laban's house in Haran. On the way to Haran, Jacob had a visitation from God, which is so profound and awesome in scope.

Gen 28:12-17
AND HE DREAMED, AND BEHOLD A LADDER SET UP ON THE EARTH, AND THE TOP OF IT REACHED TO HEAVEN: AND BEHOLD THE ANGELS OF GOD ASCENDING AND DESCENDING ON IT. And, behold, the LORD stood above it, and said, I am the LORD God of Abraham thy father, and the God of Isaac: the land whereon thou liest, to thee will I give it, and to thy seed; And thy seed shall be as the dust of the earth, and thou shalt spread abroad to the west, and to the east, and to the north, and to the south: and in thee and in thy seed shall all the families of the earth be blessed. And, behold, I am with thee, and will keep thee in all places whither thou goest, and will bring thee again into this land; for I will not leave thee, until I have done that which I have spoken to thee of. And Jacob awaked out of his sleep, and he said, Surely the LORD is in this place; and I knew it not. And he was afraid, and said, How dreadful is this place! this is none other but the HOUSE OF GOD, AND THIS IS THE GATE OF HEAVEN.

The interpretation of this dream is the key to the transformation and perfecting of the Saints and the glorification of the Church. The first thing to grasp from the metaphor of the ladder is that it is symbolic of Jesus, Who is the Way, THE ONLY WAY TO GOD! Secondly, the ladder connects heaven and earth. Jesus is the only mediator between heaven and earth. Thirdly the ladder, with its steps, signifies that there are divine steps to enter into God's presence.

Speaking the Word of God in divine order, as illustrated in the Tabernacle Prayer, is parallel to ascending the steps of the ladder into the presence of God. This type of prayer beautifully represents the process by which angels ascend and descend on our behalf. According to Psalms 103:20, angels heed only the voice of the Word of God, not our cries or opinions.

The statement Jacob made in Genesis 28:17, *"How dreadful is this place!"* signifies the **awesome power** that is available in the House of God. Jacob also said, *"this is none other than the house of God, and this is the gate of heaven"*. And Jesus said in Luke 19:46 that His house is the house of prayer!

Praying according to the Pattern of the House of God, gives us the power to go through the gate, and then up to the *"High Places"*. In the High Places spiritual warfare is accomplished more easily and effectively. In this realm we are seated with Christ in heavenly places, far above all the power of the enemy (Ephesians 1:20-21 - 2:6).

Gen 28:18-19
And Jacob rose up early in the morning, and took the STONE that he had put for his pillows, and set it up for a pillar, and poured oil upon the top of it. And he called the name of that place BETHEL: but the name of that city was called LUZ at the first.

I Peter 2:6
Wherefore also it is contained in the scripture, Behold, I lay in Sion a CHIEF CORNER STONE, elect, precious: and he that believeth on him shall not be confounded.

The stone Jacob anointed was a memorial stone for the House of God. That stone is symbolic of none other than the Chief Corner Stone of the House of God, Jesus Christ. *"Bethel"* means the House of God. Incredibly, the chain of references also takes us to the same word for ram, which was an element in the covenant of Abraham. The ram means having the strength of Almighty God. Therefore, Bethel or the House of God will give us the power to have the strength of the Almighty within us. *"Luz"* in the Hebrew means an almond tree, which prophetically means revelation knowledge and being completely awake spiritually. Praying the divine steps of the House of God will bring us into wisdom, understanding, revelation knowledge, and power as we ascend into the presence of God.

In this dream Jacob saw angels ascending and descending the ladder. They are God's emissaries on the earth, sent to minister for the heirs of salvation. They only hearken to the voice of the Word of God. They ascend the ladder of the House of God with our prayers spoken in divine order and descend to bring the manifestation to the earth realm. Jacob had a powerful revelation concerning the House of God being the House of Prayer. As we ascend into the House of God according to the Pattern (steps), we will be able to bring the eternal purposes of God into the physical realm!

Wrestling With God

Gen 32:24-30
And Jacob was left alone; and there wrestled a man with him until the breaking of the day. And when he saw that he prevailed not against him, he touched the hollow of his thigh; AND THE HOLLOW OF JACOB'S THIGH WAS OUT OF JOINT, AS HE WRESTLED WITH HIM. And he said, Let me go, for the day breaketh. And he said, I will not let thee go, EXCEPT THOU BLESS ME. And he said unto him, What is thy name? And he said, Jacob. And he said, THY NAME SHALL BE CALLED NO MORE JACOB, BUT ISRAEL: FOR AS A PRINCE HAST THOU POWER WITH GOD AND WITH MEN, AND HAST PREVAILED. And Jacob asked him, and said, Tell me, I pray thee, thy name. And he said, Wherefore is it that thou dost ask after my name? AND HE BLESSED HIM THERE. And Jacob called the name of the place Pe-ni'-el: FOR I HAVE SEEN GOD FACE TO FACE, AND MY LIFE IS PRESERVED.

It is quite easy to see why God loved Jacob. Not only did he wrestle all night long through the darkest hours, but he would not stop even though his hip had been knocked out of place. The Word says, *"his thigh was out of joint 'AS' he wrestled"*. The man wrestling with him had to ask Jacob to let him go! Jacob had such a great desire for the blessings of God that he became relentless in his pursuit. Jacob proved to God just how much he wanted the covenant blessings, by refusing to let go until he had been blessed. The man asked Jacob for his name; he then *"blessed"* Jacob by changing his name to *"Israel"*. Then we see Jacob asking the man for his name, so he could bless him also. Jacob wanted to enter into a two-way blessing denoting a covenant relationship. Then the scripture states that the man asked Jacob why he asked for his name: and the man *"blessed"* Jacob. This word *"blessed"* is different from the first reference. This word means that God *"blessed"* Jacob by being straight, on the level, and honest — MEANING THAT HE REVEALED WHO HE REALLY WAS!

The next scripture confirms this when Jacob named the place Peniel because he had seen God face-to-face and lived! There should be no doubt that Jacob encountered the Lord Himself. The word *"wrestle"* in the Hebrew surprisingly means to float away as a "vapor". It means to seize or hold as with a grapple. The word *"grapple"* means an iron claw for grasping and holding something alongside.

To *"wrestle"* is a perfect example of prayer and the essence of Praying in the Pattern of the Tabernacle! Through the gift of the Holy Spirit, we have rivers of living water in us (John 7:37-39). As we "heat" those rivers by praying the Word according to Pattern, we release vapors of true worship. These vapors ascend into heaven forming a worship cloud for God to bring rain into our lives; ANSWERED PRAYER! Here we have vapors rising as we have an iron clad hold upon God. Releasing pleasing vapors of worship unto the Father can only come from intercessors grappling with God—praying the Word of God!

When we pray according to Pattern, we have an iron clad grasp upon the Lord because He is the fulfillment of every step in the Tabernacle! Jacob wrestling with God is a prophetic snapshot of the perfect way to pray. The word *"prevail"*, in Genesis 32:28 means to attain, overcome, have power, and to stop. This type of prayer gives us the power, literally to receive and attain converts for the Kingdom of God! It also helps us to overcome the works of the devil, and have power to stop the enemy from destroying the people of God!

Genesis 32:25 states that *"he touched the hollow of his thigh"*. The word *"touch"* means to bring down, strike, and plague. The word *"hollow"* means power, also to bow down self. The word *"thigh"* means the generative parts, to produce or to procreate offspring. The word *"joint"* means to sever oneself, be alienated and out of joint.

Let's combine everything to get a prophetic picture of what God is saying to us. We will have the power to pray for and produce a Godly offspring from those who have been beaten, brought down, and plagued. There is power in Jacob to pray and affect the people that have been alienated, dislocated and have severed themselves from God! The next scriptures will shed more light on the power that is hidden in Jacob.

Gen 32:31
And as he passed over Pen-nu-el the sun rose upon him, and he HALTED upon his thigh.

The word *"halted"* means to limp as if one-sided. Jacob became one-sided upon his generative parts, or his ability to produce and procreate. If you really look back over Jacob's life you will find this is true. Throughout his entire life, he was completely focused and concerned about obtaining the covenant blessings and perpetuating them in his children.

Let's continue with verse 32 to complete this prophetic picture of the perfect intercessor.

Gen 32:32
Therefore the children of Israel eat not of the sinew which shrank, which is upon the hollow of the thigh, unto this day: because he touched the hollow of Jacob's thigh in THE SINEW THAT SHRANK.

The word *"sinew"* means a thong. A thong means a leather strip for binding and lashing. The word *"sinew"* also means to attack, invade, overcome and assemble troops. The word *"shrank"* means a sense of failure, crippled, deprive, remove and to forget. Prophetically, God is saying that Jacob has the power to bind, lash, and overcome the enemy. Jacob will assemble the Army of God, and remove their sense of failure, inability and deprivation! The manifold wisdom of God is awesome! Within Jacob is the true power of spiritual warfare!

No wonder God states that Jacob is His inheritance and the apple of His eye. When we come to the full understanding of the truth of Jacob, we will become that mighty army that God has sent His Son to achieve. Spiritually, Jacob became one-sided upon binding and overcoming the enemy and gathering the Army of God. He was also one-sided upon reaching the lost, the failed, the crippled, the forgotten, and the deprived. Wrestling with God, which is praying according to Pattern, will give you a heart for lost souls and the Army of God!

Jacob was a man who reverenced God all of his life. From birth he had a strong desire for the things of God. In reality, there wasn't any form of rebellion or irreverence of God recorded in the life of Jacob. If Jacob were out of the will of God concerning the birthright blessings, God would have told him. He never passed up the opportunity to tell Saul of his wrong deeds; neither was He beyond telling David and countless others of His displeasure. Yet God never addressed Jacob because it was prophesied before his birth that the elder shall serve the younger.

Primarily the Church has seen Jacob as a trickster and supplanter; yet Jacob produced the chosen people of God. Likewise, when we become the king-priests of the House of God, we will also produce the chosen people of God. What awesome power and responsibility has been entrusted to us! Jacob's life is a metaphor showing that prayer according to the divine order of the House of God will bring forth the power and the glory to redeem and transform His people!

The Altar Of Incense

And Lead Us Not Into Temptation, But Deliver Us From Evil

Ex 30:1-3

And thou shalt make an altar to burn incense upon: of shittim wood shalt thou make it. A cubit shall be the length thereof, and a cubit the breadth thereof; foursquare shall it be: and two cubits shall be the height thereof: the horns thereof shall be of the same. And thou shalt overlay it with pure gold, the top thereof, and the sides thereof round about, and the horns thereof; and thou shalt make unto it a crown of gold round about.

The Altar Of Incense

True Worship Shadow

This Altar was anointed with blood and oil, and a unique blend of spices was burned as incense on it while the priests were ministering in the Inner Court. The priests would sprinkle the incense upon this Altar and the fragrant cloud of perfume would permeate the veil, into the Secret Place or Holy of Holies. In John 4:23, Jesus tells us the Father is looking for *"true worshippers"*, those who will worship Him in spirit and in truth. The anointing oil symbolized worshipping the Lord in *"spirit"* and the incense symbolized worshipping Him in *"truth"*. In order to produce "true worship" these ingredients must be present. Furthermore hot coals, used to burn the sacrifice, were taken from the Brazen Altar to burn the incense. And our own "true worship" cloud will not rise without the hot coals of our committed life, in a covenant relationship with God. The Altar of Incense is the perfect shadow to the fulfillment of true worship. Worship is our highest calling and the purpose for which we were created. On this earth, we are in preparation for the *"timeless"* ministry of giving worship unto the Lord.

Anointing Oil

The anointing oil had five main ingredients, which were MYRRH, CINNAMON, CALAMUS, CASSIA and OLIVE OIL (Exodus 30:22-25). These ingredients symbolize *"five graces"* of the Holy Spirit that will transform us into true worshippers. The anointing oil was symbolic of the Holy Spirit and His nature. In order to worship the Lord in spirit, we must possess the nature and character of the Holy Spirit. The fruit of the Spirit, found in Galatians 5:22-23, reflect the nature of the Holy Spirit. However, it should also reflect the fruit of the recreated human spirit. Our fruit can only be developed or ripened by spending time in the presence of God.

As we come to the realization that we are *"love"* creatures, born of a *"LOVE"* God, we will determine to walk in the agape love of God. First Corinthians 13 states, love is the greatest fruit and it will abide throughout eternity. We need to apply to our lives these five ingredients or graces found in the anointing oil. This will cause us to walk in such love and power that we are able to produce the fruit of true worshippers. God will be able to come into His garden, the Church, and eat of our pleasant fruit (Song of Solomon 4:16).

Worship Incense

Worshipping the Lord in truth involves our heart attitudes or motivations. In Exodus 30:34, the five ingredients in the incense were stacte, onycha, galbanum, frankincense and salt. They represent *"five heart motivations or attitudes"* that are pleasing to the Lord. A characteristic of STACTE, which is the purest myrrh, is that it is free flowing. The true worshipper is spontaneous and free flowing in his relationship with God. ONYCHA comes from an aromatic deep-sea fish. As true worshippers, when we feed upon the Word of God, we become a sweet smelling fragrance unto the Lord. We should also go deep with the Lord, and come to Him with an open, honest, and transparent heart.

GALBANUM is a bitter gum used as a medicine and is symbolic of God healing our broken heart. We can bring our broken hearts and dreams and present them to the Lord as an attitude of worship. He will mend our hearts and fulfill greater dreams than we thought possible. FRANKINCENSE is a sweet smelling gum that is symbolic of Jesus. It speaks to us of purity, prayer, intercession, and righteousness. SALT, a sign of covenant, was added to temper the mixture. Salt is symbolic of speech that is pure and full of grace (Colossians 4:6).

In summary, God says come to Him with spontaneity, transparency, depth, and humility. We take these ingredients and mix them with the purity of Jesus blended with salt, which is seasoned covenant speech, to create "true worship" incense. When we worship the Lord with these five *"graces"* and *"heart attitudes"*, symbolized by the anointing oil and worship incense, our lives begin to conform to the plan and purpose of God!

The Apostle and High Priest

According to Hebrews 7:25, the perpetual ministry of Jesus, our High Priest, is to make intercession for us. He entered into the presence of God for us on the basis of His finished work on Calvary. He perfects our petitions, prayers and worship and presents them to the Father. According to Hebrews 3:1, He is the *"Apostle and High Priest of our profession"* or confession. And He is anointed to bring every word to pass that we speak, as it lines up with the Word of God.

True Worship

The Former And Latter Rain

The main reason that God desires for us to pray according to Pattern is because of the awesome power within this Prayer Pattern to bring in the end-time harvest of souls. Every harvest physical or spiritual must be accomplished by the collective power of God and man, and must also receive the two vital elements of sun and rain. In the natural man cultivates the ground, plants the seed, protects the crops, and then reaps the harvest when full grown. God supplies the sun and rain necessary for the harvest.

Likewise in the spirit realm man cultivates the ground, which is his heart by repentance. He then plants the Word of God within it, protects the Word, and then harvests that Word when it is fully-grown. According to James 5:7, *"The husbandman waiteth for the precious fruit of the earth, and hath long patience for it, until he receive the early and latter rain"*. Job 36:27 tells us that rain is poured down on the earth according to the vapor thereof. Water originates on the earth and when heated it evaporates and becomes vapor. The vapors rise and form a cloud. The cloud gets close to the sun and the light from the sun (lightning) strikes the cloud and rain falls upon the earth. Rain is dependent upon the vapor sent up. IF THERE IS NO VAPOR—THERE WILL BE NO RAIN!

Jesus told the woman at the well that if she knew the gift of God and Who was standing before her, she would ask and He would give her living water. He also said in John 7:38, that all that believe on Him, out of their innermost being shall flow rivers of living water. The word *"water"* in the Greek means to rain, especially a shower. The water that Jesus gave us is FOR THE PRODUCTION OF RAIN! When heat is applied by the worship of God, by His Word and according to Pattern, evaporation takes place and vapors are released. Evaporation will not take place if we are lukewarm, nor can evaporation take place with our own words. It can only take place by the S-O-N, the Word of God!

As we worship the Lord by His Word, the vapors of true worship rise and form a cloud. As the cloud moves closer to the S-O-N, He reaches out and strikes the cloud and blessings rain down upon the earth. TRUE WORSHIP BRINGS THE RAIN! Now let's revisit James 5:7 where it states that the *"Husbandman"* is waiting until He receives the former and latter rain. Jesus is waiting for us to send up the vapors of true worship according to the Old Testament divine order of worship as New Testament kings and priests. THE FORMER AND LATTER RAIN IS DEPENDENT UPON US! We have been waiting for God to send the former and latter rain and He has been waiting for us to send up the vapors! NO VAPOR—NO RAIN!

Joel 2:23
Be glad then, ye children of Zion, and rejoice in the Lord your God: for he hath given you the former rain moderately, and he will cause to come down for you the rain, the former rain, and the latter rain in the first month.

There are two main rainy seasons in Israel, the autumn and spring rains, separated by several months of dry weather. The autumn rain is the former rain and the spring rain is the latter rain. Since the early 1990's, the two rainy seasons have collided so now there is continual rain in Israel. The former rain was a selective rain while the latter rain covered a widespread area. The Church, spiritual Israel, prophetically parallels whatever happens in physical Israel. Right now in the Body of Christ, we have selective rain or revival, but God has promised widespread rain and a supernatural harvest after the former and latter rain fall *"together"* in the first month (Joel 2:23). New Testament king-priests sending up true worship vapors according to the

Old Testament divine order will bring about the *"collision"* of the two rains! The result will be worldwide revival and the manifest Glory of God!

Joel 2:23-25, tells us that when the former and latter rains fall together, the harvest will be plentiful even restoring the years that the locust, cankerworm, caterpillar, and palmerworm have eaten. His Spirit shall come upon all flesh, and whoever shall call upon the name of the Lord shall be delivered (Joel 2:32). Yes, the harvest depends upon us! When we realize the importance of our king-priest ministry and send up the vapors of true worship, God will send the former and latter rain!

Jerusalem, The Place Of Worship

John 4:20-22
Our fathers worshipped in this mountain; and ye say, that in Jerusalem is the place where men ought to worship. Jesus saith unto her, Woman, believe me, the hour cometh, when ye shall neither in this mountain, nor yet at Jerusalem, worship the Father. YE WORSHIP YE KNOW NOT WHAT: WE KNOW WHAT WE WORSHIP: FOR SALVATION IS OF THE JEWS.

The woman at the well makes a statement concerning the place of worship. She says that her fathers worshipped in Samaria, but the Jews say that they should worship in Jerusalem. In John 4:21, Jesus responds by telling her there would come a day when she would not worship God in Samaria or Jerusalem. But He makes a very interesting point in verse 22. Jesus tells her, in effect, that "YOU DON'T KNOW WHAT YOU ARE DOING, YOU DON'T KNOW WHAT YOU ARE WORSHIPPING! WE JEWS, KNOW WHAT WE ARE WORSHIPPING BECAUSE SALVATION IS OF THE JEWS". JESUS WAS CONFIRMING THE JEWISH WAY OF WORSHIP – and this divine order of worship brings salvation or deliverance! What did Jesus mean when He told her that she was worshipping what she did not know? If we examine the history of this woman's ancestors and their worship in Samaria, we find that her fathers were in rebellion against God. The Lord had a united kingdom of Israel under King David. His son Solomon became king at his death. After King Solomon's death, the kingdom of Israel was separated into the Northern and Southern kingdoms. Rehoboam, Solomon's son, was king of the Southern kingdom (two tribes). Jeroboam was made king of the Northern kingdom (ten tribes) and he set up idolatrous worship in the cities and hills of Samaria (I Kings 12).

According to Leviticus 23, the Jewish males were required to appear in Jerusalem three times a year to celebrate God's Feasts. They were Passover, Pentecost, and Tabernacles. Jeroboam made two golden calves and set them up in Bethel and Dan, leading the Northern tribes into idolatry (I Kings 12:29). He told them it was too much for them to go up to Jerusalem to worship, so he established a counterfeit Feast of Tabernacles. The first Feast, Passover, was a celebration of deliverance from Egypt, or the old life of bondage. Pentecost, the second Feast held fifty days later, marked the date that God gave the ten commandments (law) in the wilderness of Sinai. The Feast of Tabernacles was the third and final Feast of the year to thank God for supernatural provision in the wilderness and to celebrate the final ingathering of the harvest.

These Feasts also symbolize our spiritual walk with God and they are in the exact pattern of the Tabernacle. Passover is our salvation by the Blood of Jesus Christ (Outer Court). Pentecost is our baptism in the Holy Spirit, where He writes His laws upon our hearts (Inner Court). The Feast of Tabernacles signifies our entrance into the fullness of our king-priest ministry (Holy of Holies). And as king-priests, we worship in "spirit and in truth" and bring the rain needed for the final harvest.

The scripture states that Jeroboam imitated the Feast of Tabernacles only. Not understanding the significance, I asked the Lord why Jeroboam only imitated the Feast of Tabernacles and not the other two. His answer astounded me, He said; *"The enemy doesn't care if you get saved and filled with the Holy Spirit, because even then he is able to make many Christians ineffective. But what the enemy hates and desperately does not want, is for you to go past the Inner Court and become king-priests that go up to Heavenly Jerusalem to worship Me! Because when this happens YOU WILL BRING THE FORMER AND LATTER RAIN and the enemy's fate will be sealed!"*

Idolatrous worship was set up in Samaria in direct rebellion to worshipping God in the manner and divine order that He had set forth. Jeroboam told the Northern Tribes that it was too much for them to follow God's ordinance and go up to Jerusalem. So when you hear that voice saying *"it's too much for you to pray according to Pattern or it doesn't take all of that"*, you will certainly know the enemy's motivation! Is it any wonder that Jesus told this woman at the well that she did not know what she was worshipping?

In John 4:21, Jesus tells her there would come a time when she would not worship in Samaria or Jerusalem. In verse 23, He further states that the true worshippers would worship God in spirit and in truth. In order for us to worship God in spirit and in truth, we must understand what that really means. Let's examine what it means to worship in spirit. Jesus Christ saved us with His Blood and gave us the Holy Spirit. Worshipping God in spirit is to worship in our spirits by the grace of the Holy Spirit. Worshipping in truth is to worship Him with the Word of God (truth) according to His will. Therefore, worshipping in spirit and in truth is worshipping God in our spirit, with the truth of His Word, in divine order!

In John 4:22 Jesus said, in effect, THE JEWS HAVE THE DIVINE ORDER OF WORSHIP AND I AM THE FULFILLMENT, THE WORD OF GOD! The divine order of worship did not change only the place of worship! Because of the cross of Calvary and the gift of the Holy Spirit, we don't have to go to physical Jerusalem to worship the Lord. We can now worship God in the spirit realm in heavenly Jerusalem. Praying the Tabernacle Prayer, declaring Jesus as the fulfillment of every part of the Tabernacle, gives us the power to become true worshippers unto God!

The Father Is Seeking You!

John 4:23-24
But the hour cometh, and now is, when the true worshippers shall worship the Father in spirit and in truth: for the Father seeketh such to worship him. God is a Spirit: and they that worship him must worship him in spirit and in truth.

In John 4:23, Jesus says that the Father is seeking true worshippers who will worship Him in spirit and in truth. Are you one of the precious worshippers God is searching for to bring in the end-time harvest of souls, the precious fruit of the earth? Are you going to fulfill your calling to be a king-priest unto God, or will you let tradition and unbelief rob you of great eternal rewards? The choice is yours my friend. Yet we must warn you that the stakes are high, because hell is forever. Every second that you sleep on your calling gives the devil more souls for destruction. The price of fulfilling this call is small when compared to an eternity of hell for a lost soul. Everything you need to begin has been prepared for you. The Word says in Romans 10:6-8, the Word is near you, in your mouth and in your heart!

And Lead Us Not Into Temptation, But Deliver Us From Evil.
(Matt 6:13)

When we ask God to purge our hearts and perfect His love within us, we are asking for deliverance from the evil one. Demonic forces cannot stand against the agape love of God. Therefore, we are to walk in love, as directed by I Corinthians 13, and keep a repentant heart. It is important that we ask the Holy Spirit to come into our hearts and purge us daily. We are then assured of having a pure heart before God.

Model For Creating Your Own Prayer

6. *Purge Your Heart And Worship God In Spirit And In Truth*
FATHER CLEANSE MY HEART AND PERFECT YOUR LOVE AND THE FRUIT OF THE SPIRIT WITHIN ME

[And Lead Us Not Into Temptation, But Deliver Us From Evil]

_____
_____
_____
_____
_____
_____
_____

_____
_____
_____
_____
_____
_____
_____
_____
_____
_____
_____
_____
_____

The Prayer Pattern

Prayer:

6. The Altar Of Incense

FATHER CLEANSE MY HEART AND PERFECT YOUR LOVE AND THE FRUIT OF THE SPIRIT WITHIN ME.
[And Lead Us Not Into Temptation, But Deliver Us From Evil]

Father create in me a clean heart, O God; and renew a right spirit within me **(Ps 51:10)**. Perfect Your love in my life according to **I Cor 13**. I want the fruit of the Spirit to ripen in me **(Gal 5:22-23 - II Peter 1:5-8)**. I pray for love, joy, peace, longsuffering, gentleness, goodness, faith, meekness and temperance: balanced with the gifts of the Spirit **(I Cor 12:8-10)**. Father God, I bring You worship attitudes of spontaneity, openness, honesty, transparency, brokenness, the sweet fragrance of Jesus, and covenant speech. I ask You to come into my heart, and let the light of Your countenance purge away all that is not pleasing to You and deliver me from evil **(Ps 4:6)**. I bring to You my weaknesses, hurts, wounds, broken dreams and broken heart. I cast all of my cares upon You for You care for me **(I Peter 5:7)**. **Heb 7:25** says that Jesus is able to deliver me and ever lives to make intercession for me. Jesus is the Apostle and High Priest of my profession and confession **(Heb 3:1)**. I thank You Lord Jesus for perfecting my prayers, worship, and all that concerns me **(Ps 138:8)**. I also ask You to take the coal and cleanse my lips, for life and death are in the power of the tongue **(Prov 18:21)**. Put a guard over my mouth so that I will say only Your words of peace and prosperity over myself and others **(Col 4:6)**. Father I thank You that I have a covenant relationship with You. I am blessed of God Most High, the possessor of heaven and earth and blessed be God Most High; that has delivered all of my enemies into my hand **(Gen 14:19-20)**.

The Veil And The Secret Place

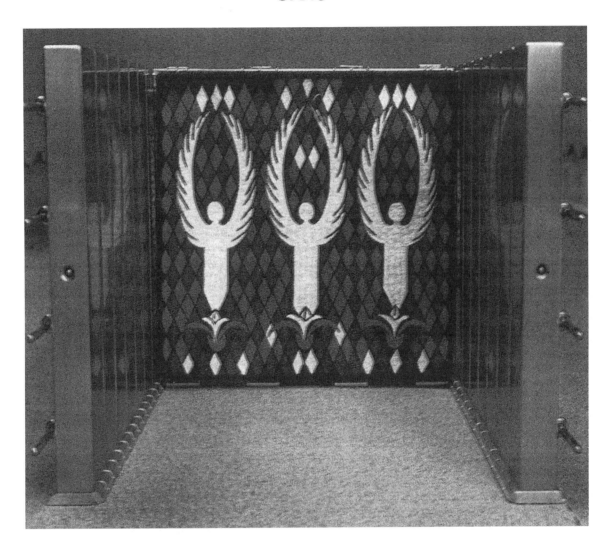

Ex 26:31

And thou shalt make a vail of blue, and purple, and scarlet,
and fine twined linen of cunning work: with
cherubims shall it be made:

The Veil Called "The Life"

Beyond The Veil

The veil of the Secret Place was made of fine linen, interwoven with three cherubim. The cherubim symbolized the fullness of the Godhead. The veil divided the Holy Place from the Holy of Holies, and guarded the entrance to the presence of God. The veil was positioned behind the Altar of Incense. The priests, in their daily ministry, would place incense upon the Altar and the cloud of fragrant perfume would permeate the veil and go into the presence of God. But only the High Priest could enter beyond the veil, and only once a year on the Day of Atonement. The earthly ministry of Jesus relates to the Outer and Inner Courts, while His heavenly ministry relates to the Secret Place.

Heb 10:20-22
By a new and living way, which he hath consecrated for us, through the veil, that is to say, his flesh; And having an high priest over the house of God; Let us draw near with a true heart in full assurance of faith, having our hearts sprinkled from an evil conscience, and our bodies washed with pure water.

After the death of Jesus, He entered into His heavenly ministry, as High Priest of the House of God (Hebrews 8:1-2). Matthew 27:51 tells us that the veil of the Temple was torn in two from *"TOP TO BOTTOM"* at the death of Jesus. This signified that the way was now open to enter God's presence! Hebrews 10:20 tells us that Jesus consecrated a *"NEW AND LIVING"* way into the presence of God for us through the *"VEIL"* of His flesh. As our High Priest, He purges our heart and conscience and draws us near to Him (Hebrews 10:22). At this point we shed the *"veil"* of our flesh, in prayer, and our spirits soar into God's presence. This is the only way for our spirits to experience complete satisfaction in this life. It is joy unspeakable and full of glory!

The Ark Of The Covenant

For Thine Is The Kingdom, And The Power, And The Glory, For Ever. A-Men.

Ps 91:1

He that dwelleth in the secret place of the most High shall abide under the shadow of the Almighty.

The Ark Of The Covenant

The Throne Of God On Earth

Ex 25:17-21
And thou shalt make a mercy seat of pure gold: two cubits and a half shall be the length thereof, and a cubit and a half the breadth thereof. And thou shalt make two cherubims of gold, of beaten work shalt thou make them, in the two ends of the mercy seat. And make one cherub on the one end, and the other cherub on the other end: even of the mercy seat shall ye make the cherubims on the two ends thereof. And the cherubims shall stretch forth their wings on high, covering the mercy seat with their wings, and their faces shall look one to another; toward the mercy seat shall the faces of the cherubims be. And thou shalt put the mercy seat above upon the ark; and in the ark thou shalt put the testimony that I shall give thee.

The Ark of the Covenant was a chest overlaid with gold within and without (Exodus 25:10-11). The cover was called the Mercy Seat, and it means, *"to atone"* or *"cover"*. This was where the blood of the sacrifice was placed on the Day of Atonement. There were Cherubim on each end of the Mercy Seat and the faces of the Cherubim looked toward one another and towards the Mercy Seat. This symbolized the Father, Son, and Holy Spirit in the work of redemption. The Mercy Seat is our Lord Jesus Christ and the Cherubim are the Father and Holy Spirit looking with favor upon the Blood sacrifice of the Son. The Ark was the throne of God on earth! Jesus kept the Law, and was obedient to God with all His heart, soul, mind, and strength. His complete compliance to the Law is credited to our account. Now when the Father looks at us, He sees us through the Blood of Jesus, thereby viewing us as perfect!!! Glory to God forever!!!

The Day Of Atonement

Once a year, on the Day of Atonement, the high priest entered the Most Holy Place with blood, sprinkled it once on the Mercy Seat and seven times before it on the ground (Leviticus 16:14). Seven is the number of perfection and fullness. The Blood of Jesus is the sum total of perfection and the fulfillment of this type and shadow. It is only the Blood of Jesus that has the power to restore all things to proper order! Once we enter God's presence, we realize that there are still things within us that do not measure up to His standards of holiness. The only way we can stand in the light of His Glory and presence is because His Blood is there on the Mercy Seat, speaking on our behalf. The Father and Holy Spirit (Cherubim) look upon the Blood of Jesus and us with complete contentment.

According to Exodus 25:22, the Lord would meet and commune with the High Priest from above the Mercy Seat between the two Cherubim. Numbers 7:89 states the voice of the Lord came from the Mercy Seat and this is where the blood was applied. Thank God the Blood of Jesus was applied to the heavenly Mercy Seat and it is always there speaking FOR US and TO US! As the Lord meets with and communes with us in the Secret Place, we get clear and distinct direction concerning our destiny in Him. Too often, we have failed to come into His presence so we can hear His voice. The Lord may not be inclined to shout to the Outer or Inner Courts, His will and purpose for our lives.

Jesus Was The Ark
The Carrier Of God's Presence

Jesus was the carrier of God's presence on the earth. In Colossians 2:9, we are told; in Him, dwelt the fullness of the Godhead (Father, Son, and Holy Spirit) bodily. We know it was God in Christ reconciling the world unto Himself.

But now we have entered into the realm where the God in Christ has become the Christ in us! As Colossians 1:27 tells us, it is Christ in us; the hope of glory! We are the treasure chests of the Lord for He has deposited the treasure of the Holy Spirit inside of us. The *"excellency of the power"* is of God and not of man (II Corinthians 4:7).

Contents Of The Ark

According to Hebrews 9:4 the contents of the Ark were as follows:

The Golden Pot Of Manna

The Ark housed the Golden Pot of Manna. It was a reminder of how God supernaturally fed the Israelites in the wilderness with Manna from heaven. It is also a reminder of the *"Hidden Manna"* or *"Bread from Heaven"* that Melchizedek gave to Abraham to cut covenant. This was God's promise that Jesus would be within us to give us the strength of the Almighty for provision, power and deliverance. According to Revelation 2:17, there is Hidden Manna that is available to him that overcomes. We must overcome the world, the flesh, and the devil to enter into our covenant relationship to be king-priests unto God.

Aaron's Rod

Aaron's Rod that blossomed was also in the Ark. It brought forth buds, blossoms, and almonds (Numbers 17:8). Almonds are symbolic of resurrection power and awakening. As king-priests we are to bud, blossom, and bring forth fruit with the resurrection power of our Lord. By praying according to Pattern, we will transform our lives and the lives of every precious stone in our breastplate.

The Tables Of The Law

The third item in the Ark was the Tables of the Law, the Ten Commandments, which were given to Moses on Mount Sinai. Under the New Covenant, God promised to write His laws in our minds and our hearts. As king-priests, we are to know and declare the Word of God according to Pattern so all will come to know Him (Hebrews 8:10-11).

Christ Entered Heaven Itself

Hebrews 9:24 states, that Christ appeared in heaven in the presence of God for us. After the resurrection of Jesus, He entered the heavenly sanctuary with His Blood and placed it on the Mercy Seat. His Blood is speaking now and forever throughout the endless ages of eternity. It is speaking of His mercies and His wonderful plan of redemption!

Pleasures Forevermore!

We can forever dwell beneath the shadow of His wings in this Secret Place. Psalms 16:11 states: *"Thou wilt shew me the path of life: in thy presence is fulness of joy; at thy right hand there are pleasures for evermore"*. The *"path of life"* is the journey through the Tabernacle into the very presence of God. There is no greater joy in life than to be in the King's presence in communion and fellowship with Him!

The Sevenfold Mercy Of God

The Mercy Of God

On the Day of Atonement the blood of the sacrifice was applied to the Mercy Seat and seven times before it, on the ground (Leviticus 16:14). After the resurrection of Jesus, He entered the heavenly sanctuary with His Blood and placed it on heaven's Mercy Seat. Hebrews 12:24 states the Blood of Jesus speaks better things than that of Abel, but we are not told what these things are.

One day in prayer I asked God what is the Blood of Jesus speaking? God replied by asking me the question; *"Where was the Blood applied?"* I said, *"On the Mercy Seat"*. He replied; *"IT SPEAKS MERCY!"* We began to study *"mercy"* and discovered that mercy is much more than we had previously thought. Psalm 136 contains a powerful sevenfold definition of mercy giving us the key to bring powerful worship to the Lamb of God for His shed Blood!

Ps 136:1-4
O give thanks unto the LORD; for he is good: for his mercy endureth for ever. O give thanks unto the God of gods: for his mercy endureth for ever. O give thanks to the Lord of lords: for his mercy endureth for ever. To him who alone doeth great wonders: for his mercy endureth for ever.

In these verses we have the identity, the **TOTAL DOMINION**, and supremacy of God in His mercy. First the scripture tells us that He is good, and the God of gods and the Lord of lords. Then it declares His supremacy by saying He alone does great wonders. The goodness, dominion and supremacy of God and His mercy have no equal.

Ps 136:5-9
To him that by wisdom made the heavens: for his mercy endureth for ever. To him that stretched out the earth above the waters: for his mercy endureth for ever. To him that made great lights: for his mercy endureth for ever: The sun to rule by day: for his mercy endureth for ever: The moon and stars to rule by night: for his mercy endureth for ever.

In these scriptures we have the awesome **CREATIVE POWER** of His mercy. This power made the heavens, the earth, the stars, the sun and the moon! Isn't it interesting to know that mercy has the power to create?

Ps 136:10-12
To him that smote Egypt in their firstborn: for his mercy endureth for ever: And brought out Israel from among them: for his mercy endureth for ever: With a strong hand, and with a stretched out arm: for his mercy endureth for ever.

Mercy killed the first born of Egypt bringing **TOTAL DELIVERANCE**. What a contrast! First we have mercy identified as being good in God's total dominion and creative power. Now we see mercy delivering God's people from bondage! Glory to God!

Ps 136:13-16
To him which divided the Red sea into parts: for his mercy endureth for ever: And made Israel to pass through the midst of it: for his mercy endureth for ever: But overthrew Pharaoh and his host in the Red sea: for his mercy endureth for ever. To him which led his people through the wilderness: for his mercy endureth for ever.

MIRACULOUS POWER is in mercy! We see God opening the Red Sea for Israel to pass through. Then we see Pharaoh and his host destroyed. We also see that God led the Israelites through the wilderness, which was in itself a miraculous feat. Their food and water was supplied supernaturally and their clothing never wore out!

Ps 136:17-20
To him which smote great kings: for his mercy endureth for ever: And slew famous kings: for his mercy endureth for ever: Sihon king of the Amorites: for his mercy endureth for ever: And Og the king of Bashan: for his mercy endureth for ever:

Mercy **DESTROYS OUR ENEMIES!** Just as there are ranks in a physical army, there are ranks in the spiritual realm. Kings are the highest rank. *"Sihon king of the Amorites"* means a violent spirit with evil influence. *"Og king of Bashan"* denotes a demonic spirit of pride and arrogance. The mercy of God destroys these demonic influences over our lives.

Ps 136:21-22
And gave their land for an heritage: for his mercy endureth for ever: Even an heritage unto Israel his servant: for his mercy endureth for ever.

We have the manifestation of **COVENANT BLESSINGS** through His mercy. Mercy also gives us the power to rule with the authority of God. As we learned earlier the name *"Israel"* means to rule as God, and like Him we speak the Word and see it manifested. In essence mercy will bring the manifestation of covenant blessings and our spiritual inheritance.

Ps 136:23-26
Who remembered us in our low estate: for his mercy endureth for ever: And hath redeemed us from our enemies: for his mercy endureth for ever. Who giveth food to all flesh: for his mercy endureth for ever. O give thanks unto the God of heaven: for his mercy endureth for ever.

These scriptures highlight the **GRACE** that is in the mercy of God. First we are remembered in our low estate and are rescued from all our enemies. Then we find that mercy brings forth the provision for all of God's creation. This is truly unmerited favor, kindness, and compassion. The mercy of God is sevenfold and it brings *dominion*, *creative power*, *deliverance*, *miracles, destruction of enemies*, *covenant blessings* and the *grace* of God. The mercies of God are outstanding and they are renewed every morning! At the Mercy Seat we worship the Father, Son, and Holy Spirit for the sevenfold mercies of the Blood of Jesus. Now that we know what the Blood speaks on our behalf, we can come into agreement with it, and declare it in worship. As we do this we activate the awesome power of the Blood of Jesus in our lives! Worthy is the Lamb of God!

The Sevenfold Mercy Of God

As the Blood of Jesus was applied to the Mercy Seat,
Our redemption was made perfect, full, and complete.
The Blood of Jesus speaks *"MERCY"* and the story is yet untold,
That the Lord's mercy endures forever and it is sevenfold!

The Lord is good, and His mercy endures forever, it's clear and it's plain,
His **DOMINION** is from everlasting to everlasting, and He will reign.
The Lord is good, and His mercy endures forever, is the word for this hour,
The mercy of God embraces His awesome **CREATIVE POWER**.
The Lord is good, and His mercy endures forever, against any circumstance,
With a mighty hand and outstretched arm, mercy brings **DELIVERANCE.**

The Lord is good, and His mercy endures forever, it meets all of our needs,
The mercy of God shows forth His glory in **MIRACULOUS** deeds.
The Lord is good, and His mercy endures forever, all the world will see,
Through our Mighty Man of War, mercy **DESTROYS** all of our enemies.
The Lord is good, and His mercy endures forever, our provision we receive,
It will bring the **COVENANT BLESSINGS** to those who will believe.
The Lord is good, and His mercy endures forever, we will all say,
The **GRACE** of God is upon us, because mercy made the way.

As the Blood of Jesus was applied to the heavenly Mercy Seat,
Our redemption was made perfect, full, and complete.
The Blood of Jesus speaks *"MERCY"* and the story has just been told,
That the Lord's mercy endures forever and it is sevenfold!

The Triune Anointing

Heb 9:3-5
And after the second veil, the tabernacle which is called the Holiest of all; which had the golden censer, and the ark of the covenant overlaid round about with gold, wherein was the golden pot that had manna, and Aaron's rod that budded, and the tables of the covenant; And over it the cherubims of glory shadowing the mercyseat; of which we cannot now speak particularly.

The Ark of the Covenant was a golden *"treasure"* chest that housed three items that were proof of the covenant promises God made to Israel. The first item was the Golden Pot of Manna representing how God supernaturally fed the Israelites in the wilderness with Manna from heaven. The second item was Aaron's rod that blossomed representing the power of a holy priesthood to bring about restoration. The third item was the Tables of the Law, which Moses received at Mount Sinai, representing the Word of God.

These three items were symbolic of the offices of the king, priest and prophet. Jesus, the King-Priest-Prophet, desires every believer to walk in this triune anointing. The Golden Pot of Manna was symbolic of the office of the Prophet. **Jesus, the Prophet**, was the *"Bread of Life"* or *"True Manna"* for the world. We are to be His **prophets**, filled with Manna, feeding lost souls by proclaiming the Gospel to all men. The **Priesthood of Jesus** was found in the Rod of Aaron that miraculously brought forth buds, blossoms and fruit displaying resurrection power. Jesus, as the Priest of God, had resurrection power to raise the dead, heal all manner of disease, and cast out demons. As His **priests**, we blossom and bear fruit with this same power through intercession and communion with God. The Tables of the Law represented the **Kingship of Jesus**. He was the Living Word, Who spoke the oracles of God. As His **kings,** we declare and decree the Word of God and establish it upon this earth, to manifest His awesome power and presence!

For Thine Is The Kingdom, And The Power, And The Glory, For Ever. Amen.
(Matt 6:13)

We come into the Holy of Holies to exalt the Father, Son, and Holy Spirit. The Lord Jesus brought the Kingdom of God to the earth. The Holy Spirit brought the power of God to every believer and the Father will bring the glory that will cover the earth as the waters cover the sea. When we declare God's total dominion and supremacy, we establish it in our lives and upon the earth.

Model For Creating Your Own Prayer

7. Worship The Father, Son And Holy Spirit

FATHER THANK YOU FOR LETTING ME COME INTO YOUR HOLY PRESENCE.

[For Thine Is The Kingdom, And The Power, And The Glory, For Ever. A-Men.]

_____
_____
_____
_____
_____
_____
_____
_____
_____
_____
_____
_____
_____

The Prayer Pattern

Prayer:

7.   The Ark Of The Covenant

FATHER THANK YOU FOR LETTING ME COME INTO YOUR HOLY PRESENCE.
[For Thine Is The Kingdom, And The Power, And The Glory, For Ever. A-Men.]

You have shown me the path of life: in Your presence is fullness of joy; at Your right hand there are pleasures for evermore **(Ps 16:11)**. Daddy thank You for the precious Blood of Jesus that is speaking from the Mercy Seat, proclaiming greater things than that of Abel **(Heb 12:24)**. I am so grateful Daddy, that when You look at me, You do not see me, but You see Jesus. Daddy God, thank You for making me a vessel that is filled with Your presence **(Col 1:27)**. Your Laws are written upon my heart and in my mind **(Heb 8:10)**. I speak and declare the truth of Your Word. I have revelation knowledge, and bud, blossom and bring forth fruit in resurrection power. The fruit and the gifts of the Spirit are operating in my life in perfect balance. I am like the Ark, a golden vessel, filled with Your covenant promises and with Your glory **(Isa 60:1-3)**. I worship You Daddy as the Giver and the Source of all life. I worship You Holy Spirit and I thank You for being the lover of my soul, my Comforter and my closest friend. I worship You Lord Jesus, for You are the King of Glory, the Lord of Hosts, Captain of heaven's armies, and the Lord strong and mighty **(Ps 24:7)**. I declare that Jesus is Lord, and His dominion is everlasting. For thine is the kingdom, the power and the glory for ever and ever, Amen.

The Abrahamic Covenant

The Covenant To Make Us Kings And Priests!

Chapter 23

The Abrahamic Covenant

In this section you will learn the true meaning of the Covenant of Abraham. We have been taught that it is a covenant of blessing—and it is. But it also has a greater and a more profound meaning that has been hidden until now. In this study of the Abrahamic Covenant, you will discover that it is a "holy covenant" to make us kings and priests unto God!

After reading this section you will know beyond a shadow of a doubt that you have a royal priesthood awaiting your reception. It is a divine wake-up call that will bring the paradigm shift needed to manifest the presence of God. Your royal priesthood is not a metaphor, nor is it a theory. It is literally the desired destiny of the Father for each of us. James 5:7 tells us that *"the husbandman waiteth for the precious fruit of the earth"*. We are so glad that He added *"and hath long patience for it!"* Let's not keep Him waiting any longer!

Melchizedek

If you ask most Christians where their covenant is located in the Bible they would tell you Genesis 12. As glorious as that portion of scripture is, it is an account of the promises and not the actual covenant. In the Old Testament most covenants contained a meal, an oath, and a blood sacrifice or the mingling of blood. These elements are found in Genesis 14 and 15. Let's begin our study in Genesis 14:18-20.

Gen 14:18-20
And Melchizedek KING of Salem brought forth bread and wine: and he was the PRIEST of the most high God. And he blessed him, and said, Blessed be Abram of the most high God, possessor of heaven and earth: And blessed be the most high God, which hath delivered thine enemies into thy hand. And he gave him tithes of all.

The first major point to note is that Melchizedek was a KING AND A PRIEST. The second major point is that no one else in the entire Bible was ever described as being the priest of the Most High God. Even Moses, a man dear to God, with whom He spoke to face to face was never described in that manner. The rule of *"first mention"* is always very significant, but the title *"THE PRIEST OF THE MOST HIGH GOD"* holds first, last and only mention! To get a clearer understanding of who Melchizedek really was, let's go to the book of Hebrews, the seventh chapter.

Heb 7:1-3
For this Melchisedec, king of Salem, priest of the most high God, who met Abraham returning from the slaughter of the kings, and blessed him; To whom also Abraham gave a tenth part of all; first being by interpretation King of righteousness, and after that also King of Salem, which is, King of peace; WITHOUT FATHER, WITHOUT MOTHER, WITHOUT DESCENT, HAVING NEITHER BEGINNING OF DAYS, NOR END OF LIFE; BUT MADE LIKE UNTO THE SON OF GOD; ABIDETH A PRIEST CONTINUALLY.

God has given us powerful clues regarding the importance of Melchizedek. He begins by emphasizing the subject stating *"this Melchizedec"*. He interprets the name and also tells us to consider how great this man was. Furthermore, He presents us with the most spectacular description that can only be compared to the Godhead. No human has a resume like this: WITHOUT FATHER OR MOTHER, HAVING NEITHER BEGINNING OF DAYS NOR END OF LIFE, BUT MADE LIKE UNTO THE SON OF GOD; ABIDETH A PRIEST CONTINUALLY. If not for this description in Hebrews, we may have been able to conclude that he was an ordinary human, but NOT WITH THIS KIND OF REPORT!

Furthermore, the interpretation of his name means *"King of righteousness"*, *"King of Salem, which is, King of peace"*. It is not only capitalized giving great honor. But it is beyond human capacity! The highest title a human king ever attained was to be king over a geographical area or nation of people, never a characteristic of the Almighty God! MELCHIZEDEK WAS THE HOLY GHOST – appearing in the form of a man!

Before we continue to bring forth this revelation, it is necessary to follow the word through to its root meaning. This can mean following a chain of references that would be too cumbersome to list. We suggest you take the time to study this in a Bible Concordance on your own; the full interpretation will bless you tremendously and increase your revelation. But for this book, we will highlight and paraphrase the interpretations. In the Greek, Melchizedek means a Patriarch. A patriarch is a father, the male leader of a family or tribe as in Abraham, Isaac, and Jacob. It is someone regarded as the founder or original head of an enterprise, organization, or tradition. It is also one who is a high dignitary of the priesthood empowered to invoke blessings.

In the Hebrew, Melchizedek means, one who has the power to bring righteousness, make right, make amends, cleanse and to justify. His name also denotes a royal king that has the power to ascend the throne and INDUCT INTO ROYALTY, AND SET UP OR MAKE KINGS AND QUEENS! He is someone who bestows the natural, moral or legal right to have prosperity. Melchizedek was also the King of Salem. Salem means peace, perfected, whole, prosperous, restore, and reward.

"THIS MELCHIZEDEK" came to make us KINGS AND PRIESTS unto God! He also came to bless us with righteousness, wholeness, peace, and prosperity! Another important point to consider is that Melchizedek belonged to *"another tribe"* (Hebrews 7:13). The priesthood of Melchizedek and Jesus Christ came from a different tribe, which was from heaven not earth. God, not man, gave their priesthood to them with an oath.

Heb 7:21
For those priests were made without an oath; but this with an oath by him that said unto him, The Lord sware and will not repent, Thou art a priest for ever after THE ORDER OF MELCHISEDEC:

Gen 14:18-19
And Melchizedek king of Salem brought forth BREAD AND WINE: and he was the priest of the most high God. And he BLESSED him, and said, BLESSED be Abram of the most high God, possessor of heaven and earth:

Our definition of the word *"blessed"* is nothing like the Hebrew definition. This word is so interesting it will astound you to know all that pertains to it. *"Bless"* means to kneel; to bless God as an act of adoration, and vice-versa; man as a benefit. It also means to abundantly bless, congratulate, kneel, praise, salute and to thank. Furthermore, it means by euphemism to curse god or the king, as treason.

At first when I read this, all I could see were the words *"to curse god or the king as treason"*. I thought I had totally missed it! This can't be true because the Holy Spirit would not have anything to do with cursing God or treason. God asked me; *"who is the god of this world?"* When I answered that satan is, I began to see the logic. Melchizedek, in a covert operation, came to officiate a holy covenant with Abraham to destroy the god of this world and to take back all that he has stolen from man. What a powerful word! That quickly settled the matter and I moved on to see the powerful meaning within this definition. Abraham knelt as an act of adoration and worship. The phrases *"vice-versa and man as a benefit"*, tells us there were two-way blessings being given. God was blessing Abraham and he was blessing God. Each party was declaring their covenant promises!

Next we have Melchizedek declaring that Abraham is blessed of the Most High God, possessor of heaven and earth. That means Abraham was blessed with spiritual and physical blessings. Then he declared blessed be God, which has delivered Abraham's enemies into his hand. Not only was there a covenant being made to bless Abraham but there was also a covenant being made to destroy his enemies! The word *"euphemism"* in the explanation of *"bless"*, means to substitute a mild word for one considered offensive. For example Melchizedek, declaring that all Abraham's enemies would be placed in his hand was a mild way of saying that God was going to annihilate every one of them! There was two-fold power being released in this covenant, one to bless Abraham and the other to destroy the god of this world!

This definition of the word *"blessed"* leaves our previous understanding of that word far behind. Actually to *"bless"* means we declare covenant words to God in worship and He declares and releases His covenant blessings upon us! Praying in the pattern of the Tabernacle is a perfect way to accomplish this. We declare and decree His Word as king-priests and Jesus, our High Priest, decrees and confers covenant blessings upon us, thereby destroying our enemies! For example: declaring that by His stripes we are healed, Jesus confirms that Word and sends forth the healing and of course when He does all spirits of infirmity are defeated!

The Bread And Wine From Heaven

Gen 14:18
And Melchizedek king of Salem brought forth bread and wine: and he was the priest of the most high God.

Melchizedek was not bringing food for Abraham, but Holy Communion elements to cut covenant. In order to understand this holy covenant, we must know the true meaning of the bread and the wine. Jesus said in Matthew 26:28, the wine they drank in communion was the Blood He shed for the remission of sins. The Hebrew definition of *"bread"* takes us through six references and its complete meaning is amazing! It begins by calling it food, bread, shewbread, also the grain for making it. The Hebrew definition of *"bread"* means to war, battle, prevail, overcome and be delivered. It also means to **BUILD THE FAMILY AND THE HOUSE OF GOD!** In the Greek it means to forgive sin, remove and take away. Clearly this describes our Lord and Savior Jesus Christ--the Bread from Heaven! He is the only one that can bring deliverance, give us the power to overcome our enemies and build the House of God.

The most important and glorious aspect of this covenant is the fact that it is completely impossible for it to fail! Melchizedek brought down the **"Bread from Heaven"**, which is symbolic of Jesus, and fed it to Abraham and then cut covenant! It cannot fail because God cut the covenant with JESUS CHRIST IN ABRAHAM!

Gal 3:16
Now to Abraham and his seed were the promises made. He saith not, And to seeds, as of many; but as of one, AND TO THY SEED, WHICH IS CHRIST.

God cut covenant with Jesus Christ, the **"Living Bread"**, Whom He knew would not break the covenant. Abraham could have blown it, but not Jesus!

Now we can fully understand the Hebrew definition of the *"bread"*. Jesus is our nourishment strength and power to do battle, prevail and overcome every foe within and without. He is the "Children's Bread of Deliverance!" Without a doubt, it was Jesus Christ with Whom the covenant was made and relied upon.

John 6:32-33
Then Jesus said unto them, Verily, verily, I say unto you, Moses gave you not that bread from heaven; but my Father giveth you the true bread from heaven. For the bread of God is he which cometh down from heaven, and giveth life unto the world.

God temporarily lost the world to satan through Adam. Do you really think He was going to put our entire existence totally upon the shoulders of fallen man? NO! Praise God for His manifold wisdom, because we see in Genesis 16 that Abraham began to go astray by not adhering to the covenant promise that Sarah would have a child. That's why God swore by Himself, to bring this covenant to pass and **HE DID; HE SWORE BY JESUS!**

Heb 6:13-14
For when God made promise to Abraham, because he could swear by no greater, HE SWARE BY HIMSELF, Saying, surely blessing I will bless thee, and multiplying I will multiply thee.

This was a holy covenant that involved the entire Godhead! Melchizedek, the Holy Spirit, brought Jesus the Bread and Wine from heaven and God the Father sealed the covenant with an oath! All God needed from Abraham was his faith, to believe Him. He did not need his brilliance or his strength. It is exactly the same today. All God needs is our faith in Him and His Word and He will do the rest!

The covenant was made with Jesus Christ, Who lives within you. If you do your part of the covenant, **IT WILL BE IMPOSSIBLE FOR YOU TO FAIL OR LOSE.** You have the awesome power of the King of Glory inside of you, backed by a sworn oath from Almighty God and total guidance from the Holy Spirit! All you have to do is bless the Lord by speaking covenant words to Him according to Pattern. Let God arise and His enemies be scattered.

Hallelujah! The only hope the devil had was to keep us in the dark about our true covenant. He didn't want us to know that we are king-priests blessed of the Most High God, anointed to destroy his works and to possess this earth for the Glory of God!

The Cutting Of The Covenant

Gen 15:9-10
And he said unto him, Take me an HEIFER of three years old, and a SHE GOAT of three years old, and a RAM of three years old, and a TURTLE DOVE, and a YOUNG PIGEON. And he took unto him all these, and divided them in the midst, and laid each piece one against another: but the BIRDS divided he not.

Gen 15:17-18
And it came to pass, that, when the sun went down, and it was dark, behold a SMOKING FURNACE, AND A BURNING LAMP that passed between those pieces. In the same day the LORD made a covenant with Abram, saying, Unto thy seed have I given this land, from the river of Egypt unto the great river, the river Euphrates:

God told Abraham to gather particular elements for the actual cutting of the covenant. Notice verse 10 says, that he took them and divided them in the midst and laid each piece one against another; but the birds were not divided. Prophetically God is saying that He had the heifer, the she-goat, and the ram divided in half and placed them against one another because all of these elements represent our desperate need for Jesus. We cannot be perfected without Jesus, the *"Smoking Furnace and Burning Lamp – The Torch"*, coming in the midst of us.

Yet the turtledove, symbolic of the Holy Spirit, was not divided because God has purposed for us to walk in the full power of the Holy Spirit. The young pigeon had no feathers, due to the fact that his feathers were plucked and stripped off. Therefore it was symbolic of us losing our *"coats of glory"* through Adam's sin. It also was not divided because God has declared that we will recover all that the devil has stolen from us. We will recover our glory, wealth, and dominion, not half but ALL! Glory to the only wise God for His blessed covenant!

We must believe the Word of God to the point, that absolutely nothing will make us doubt it. We are to win the nations and we are not going to do it powerless and broke. Nor will it happen by just wishing it to happen! We must take up our king-priest duties, declare and war for it according to Pattern. We must uproot every lie of the enemy that speaks against our covenant right to be anointed, wealthy, and victorious over the devil. Many people are dying and going to hell because we, the Body of Christ, are not showing the world the power of the gospel.

Our Melchizedek Priesthood

Ps 110:1-4
The LORD said unto my Lord, Sit thou at my right hand, until I make thine enemies thy footstool. The LORD shall send the rod of thy strength out of Zion: rule thou in the midst of thine enemies. Thy PEOPLE SHALL BE WILLING IN THE DAY OF THY POWER, in the beauties of holiness from the womb of the morning: thou hast the dew of thy youth. THE LORD HATH SWORN, AND WILL NOT REPENT, THOU ART A PRIEST FOR EVER AFTER THE ORDER OF MELCHIZEDEK.

The Psalmist records the Father speaking to the Messiah. In Verse 4 God the Father has sworn with an oath that Jesus is a Priest after the Order of Melchizedek. First of all it simply makes sense that the Messiah COULD ONLY BE AFTER THE ORDER OF SOMEONE WHO WAS GOD HIMSELF (THE HOLY GHOST). Therefore we are kings and priests after the pattern the Lord Himself established and we also have a *"Melchizedek priesthood"*. In Verse 3 God is talking about us; His people, WILLING TROOPS, READY ON THE DAY OF BATTLE! And we are coming forth *"in the beauties of holiness";* which is translated as wearing our PRIESTLY GARMENTS!

It is time to become the king-priests that God has called us to be. THE COVENANT PROMISES MADE TO ABRAHAM LAID THE FOUNDATION TO MAKE US KING AND PRIESTS! The Lamb of God came as a KING AND PRIEST, and fulfilled the Abrahamic Covenant promises by shedding His precious Blood. And by His Blood we have been made KINGS AND PRIESTS! Therefore, we are destined to be the anointed, wealthy, glorious and victorious Church that Jesus so lovingly laid down His life to create!

Feasts Of The Lord And The Tabernacle

Passover – Outer Court

Pentecost – Inner Court

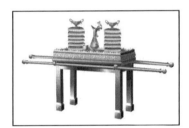

Feast of Tabernacles – Holy Of Holies

The Feasts Of The Lord

The Feasts Of The Lord And Your Royal Priesthood

I Peter 2:9
But ye are a chosen generation, a royal priesthood, an holy nation, a peculiar people; that ye should shew forth the praises of him who hath called you out of darkness into his marvellous light:

In this scripture we are told that we are a royal priesthood and a holy nation to *"shew"* forth the praises of God. As we learned earlier, our covenant is a covenant to enter into this royal priesthood. Therefore, it is our duty to know and declare the things that God has done, is doing, and will do. The perfect description of the Lord and all He has come to accomplish is found in the Tabernacle. As king-priests, we are to declare and decree the praises of our Lord Jesus Christ according to the Pattern of the Tabernacle.

Another important aspect of our priesthood is the understanding and celebration of the Feasts of the Lord.

Leviticus 23:1-2
And the LORD spake unto Moses, saying, Speak unto the children of Israel, and say unto them, Concerning the Feasts of the LORD, which ye shall proclaim to be holy convocations, EVEN THESE ARE MY FEASTS.

Lev 23:4
THESE ARE THE FEASTS OF THE LORD, even holy convocations, which ye SHALL PROCLAIM IN THEIR SEASONS

As New Testament priests, we are to understand the Jewish culture and traditions of celebrating these holy days. Why? The word *"Feasts"* in the Hebrew means holy appointments with God! These are the Father's HOLY APPOINTED TIMES to meet with us and release His blessings. The Lord makes it plain that these are NOT THE FEASTS OF ISRAEL, THEY ARE HIS FEASTS! So we should not treat them as if they are unimportant. Additionally, the word *"convocations"* mean rehearsals. These Feasts or holy appointed times are prophetic rehearsals of what God has done or will do in the future.

Three times a year *(Passover, Pentecost, Tabernacles),* Jewish males were REQUIRED to appear before the Lord in Jerusalem (Deut. 16:16). JESUS CELEBRATED THE FEASTS! And in the four gospels we find that during each Feast His actions and teachings were relating powerful truths. We can only fully understand them in their correct context, background or framework of the Feast being celebrated. In other words, we can more fully absorb the meaning of what Jesus is saying and doing in their correct settings, as we understand the Feasts.

Leviticus 23:4 tells us, we are to *"proclaim these Feasts in their seasons".* This means the Lord wants us to "DECLARE or SAY" something concerning each rehearsal! After you discover the date of each celebration, ask the Holy Spirit how He wants you to observe or celebrate them. We cannot technically "keep" the Feasts as the Israelites did when there was a Temple in Jerusalem. But we can celebrate these holy appointments as we are led by the Holy Spirit. Above all, He would like you to pray over the earth during these special times. We have been totally blessed and in awe during each celebration from the wisdom, love, revelation and prayer that the Holy Spirit brings forth during these special seasons.

The Feasts of the Lord represent a prophetic timeline for the Church as well as phases in the life of the believer. But it is also interesting to note these Feasts follow the Pattern of the Tabernacle of Moses.

The **Feast of Passover** exemplifies the Brazen Altar. This is where we receive total deliverance by the Blood of the Lamb of God. The Brazen Laver represents the **Feast of Unleavened Bread** and **First Fruits.** It is here that we are separated and consecrated unto God by the washing of the water by the Word. The Candlestick, Table of Shewbread and Altar of Incense symbolize the **Feast of Pentecost**. We are anointed and illuminated with the power of the Holy Spirit at the Candlestick. We become intercessors and have communion with God at the Table of Shewbread. Next, we enter into worship in spirit and in truth at the Altar of Incense.

The Church has fulfilled the first two Feast seasons, which are Passover and Pentecost. The Lamb of God died on Passover and the Holy Spirit was sent on the Day of Pentecost. And there have also been prophetic fulfillments to both. The next Feast to be fulfilled is Tabernacles. The Feast of Tabernacles is identified with the Holy of Holies and the Ark of the Covenant. The **Feast of Trumpets** will be fulfilled when we understand and declare and decree our covenant. A shofar or ram's horn used as the trumpet for this Feast is symbolic of the Abrahamic Covenant when God supplied the ram for the sacrifice instead of Isaac. In essence, to blow the trumpet, means to "DECLARE OUR COVENANT". We will fulfill this prophetic picture by becoming king-priests and declaring our covenant promises. And by praying according to Pattern, we will birth an attitude of repentance and restoration as displayed on the **Day of Atonement**. We will then complete the **Feast of Tabernacles**, with a great harvest of souls, and we will enter into the final rest of God! Glory to His Wonderful Name!!!

The Feasts Of The Lord

The Israelites Celebrated The Three Major Feasts Of The Lord And They Were Divided Into Seven Parts.

The Feasts Of The Lord Also Perfectly Correspond To The Pattern Of The Tabernacle Of Moses.

Passover - Mar/Apr - Outer Court
(Salvation By The Blood Of Jesus)

- **Passover** - Celebration of the deliverance of the Israelites from bondage.
- **Unleavened Bread** - Celebration of the separation from the old life.
- **First Fruits** - Consecration of the first fruits of the barley harvest.

Pentecost - May/Jun - Inner Court
(Baptism In The Holy Spirit)

- **Pentecost** - Celebration marking the completion of the wheat harvest and a memorial to the Israelites receiving the Law, Statutes, and Tabernacle Pattern.

Tabernacles - Sep/Oct - Holy of Holies
(Fullness Of King-Priest Ministry)

- **Trumpets** - New Year and time of preparing the people for the Day of Atonement.
- **Day of Atonement** - The day of national repentance and cleansing from sin.
- **Tabernacles** - Celebration of God's supernatural provision in the wilderness and the future hope of entering His rest. It was also a celebration of the final ingathering of the fruit harvest.

Elijah

Mal 4:4-6
Remember ye the law of Moses my servant, which I commanded unto him in Horeb for all Israel, with the statutes and judgments. Behold, I will send you Elijah the prophet before the coming of the great and dreadful day of the LORD: And he shall turn the heart of the fathers to the children, and the heart of the children to their fathers, lest I come and smite the earth with a curse.

Before we begin our study of Elijah, we must lay a foundation that will help our understanding of the prophetic significance of his life. Elijah was a Prophet of God commissioned to revive the Law of Moses and the covenant in the hearts of the Israelites. In other words, Elijah was to bring a revival of *"true worship"* to the Heavenly Father. Our commission as king-priests is the same as that of Elijah. We are to bring a revival of true worship to the Heavenly Father upon this earth!

The Apostolic And Prophetic Anointing

Elijah was an *"apostolic"* Prophet who established the will and order of God in the land. Elijah also moved in an anointing and power that was astounding. It is time for us to take a good look at this power and the message that God has placed inside of the life of Elijah. Let's begin by looking at where we are, as a Church, in regard to the anointing.

Eph 4:11-13
And he gave some, apostles; and some, prophets; and some, evangelists; and some, pastors and teachers; For the perfecting of the Saints, for the work of the ministry, for the edifying of the body of Christ: Till we all come in the unity of the faith, and of the knowledge of the Son of God, unto a perfect man, unto the measure of the stature of the fulness of Christ:

For the last 2,000 years the Church has been, in most cases, three-dimensional. We have recognized the ministry of the Evangelist, Pastor and Teacher. Ephesians 4:11-13 describes five ministry gifts that are to equip and bring the Body of Christ to perfection. In these last days God is restoring the ministry of the Apostle and Prophet.

The Apostle has *"breakthrough"* anointing and the ability to establish and bring order. The Prophet has the ability to *"hear the voice of the Lord and to declare His Word"*. The apostolic and prophetic anointings are in the process of being restored to the Church to make it complete.

Every believer should have the benefit of these five anointings. This does not mean that he will hold these offices, but each should have the uniqueness of each anointing operating in his life. This can be achieved by praying the Word of God according to Pattern. When we pray according to Pattern, we will find that we have the breakthrough anointing of the Apostle, and we will declare the Word of God as the Prophet. We become a Pastor, Evangelist, and Teacher, exercising the power to evangelize the world from our prayer closet! Elijah was a Prophet but he also had all of these anointings manifested in him. He ministered to Israel as the Apostle, the Prophet, the Pastor, the Teacher and the Evangelist and brought down the Glory of God! This is the fullness that God wants to bring to pass in each of us!

Elijah comes on the scene with no recorded genealogy, only an introduction as *"Elijah the Tishbite"*. Elijah's name means *"beloved of Yah"*, and Tishbite means *"converter"*. Yah is God's covenant name. Elijah's name means to return to the covenant of God. His commission was to turn the children's hearts to their heavenly Father. Malachi 4:4 begins with *"remember ye the law of Moses my servant"*, which means the Tabernacle of God or His prescribed method of approach to Him. Verse 5 states, *"I will send Elijah the Prophet"*, which the Israelites understood to mean that he would come before the Messiah. In other words, God will send Elijah the Prophet to make us remember the Tabernacle of Moses!

Matt 17-10-11
And his disciples asked him, saying, Why then say the scribes that Elias must first come? And Jesus answered and said unto them, ELIAS TRULY SHALL FIRST COME, AND RESTORE ALL THINGS.

The disciples of Jesus asked Him in Matthew 17:10, *"Why then say the scribes that Elias must first come?"* In verse 11, Jesus said that Elijah must come and *"restore all things"*. He goes on to say in verse 12 that John the Baptist was Elijah, meaning he came in the *"spirit and power"* of Elijah to bring repentance and restoration.

Just as John the Baptist came to prepare the way of the Lord the first time, the king-priests of God empowered with the apostolic and prophetic anointings are the *"Elijahs"* that will prepare the way for His Second Coming! But notice the order of Malachi 4:4-5, REMEMBERING THE LAW OF MOSES OR THE TABERNACLE WILL PRECEDE THIS REVIVAL! *"The Elijah Anointing"* will make the Church *"remember"* the Law of Moses and usher in the Glory of God!

This *"new breed"* of Christian will pick up the prayer mantle of Elijah and go forth in his spirit and power to restore all things by their intercession through the Tabernacle. They will change the hearts of men and produce true worshippers who know *"Abba Father"*, *"Daddy God"*, in pure fellowship and intimacy. The true worship will produce a cloud of fragrant perfume that will rise to the Father, and as stated before, the true worship cloud will bring the former and latter rain!

Another powerful key Elijah gave us is reproduction. We are to reproduce ourselves just as Elijah reproduced himself in Elisha. The reproduction of king-priests is beneficial to all because there is no competition. The more king-priests we have, the more power, glory, honor and rain for all of us!

There Will Be No Rain

I Kin 17:1-4
And Elijah the Tishbite, who was of the inhabitants of Gilead, said unto Ahab, As the LORD God of Israel liveth, before whom I stand, there shall not be dew nor rain these years, but according to my word. And the word of the LORD came unto him, saying, Get thee hence, and turn thee eastward, and hide thyself by the brook Cherith, that is before Jordan. And it shall be, that thou shalt drink of the brook; and I have commanded the ravens to feed thee there.

In the Northern kingdom of Israel, Ahab and Jezebel were reigning and had led the people into the worship of baal. They were very evil and Jezebel had the prophets of the Lord murdered. The Lord sent Elijah to tell Ahab of His impending judgment upon the land. The word of the Lord to Ahab was that there would be no rain but according to the word of Elijah. At that time, the worshippers of these idols thought their gods controlled the weather. God chose a drought to show them Who really was in control of the weather! In I Kings 17:2-7, the Lord told Elijah to go to Cherith, which means to *"cut covenant"*. It was here that God supernaturally fed him and took care of all of his needs. Today, our power comes from knowing our covenant to be king-priests unto the Lord, and then He will supernaturally care for us.

The Widow Of Zarephath

I Kin 17:8-9
And the word of the LORD came unto him, saying, Arise, get thee to Zarephath, which belongeth to Zidon, and dwell there: behold, I have commanded a widow woman there to sustain thee.

The Lord directed Elijah to a widow in Zarephath, who would sustain him until He was ready to bring rain upon the earth. As we all know God made supernatural provision for Elijah, the widow, and her son throughout the drought. During this time the widow's son became sick and died, however this incident demonstrates to us the awesome power that Elijah walked in.

I Kin 17:21-22
And he stretched himself upon the child three times, and cried unto the LORD, and said, O LORD my God, I pray thee, let this child's soul come into him again. And the LORD HEARD THE VOICE OF ELIJAH; and the soul of the child came into him again, and he revived.

Prior to this incident, there was no account of anyone being raised from the dead. But Elijah stretched himself upon the child three times, and prayed for his soul to return to him. The scripture says; *the Lord heard the voice of Elijah"*. God will always hear and respond to the **"voice of the prophetic"**. The prophetic voice on the earth brings life out of death. In verse 24, it is fascinating to note that the woman responds by saying: *"now by this I know that thou art a man of God, and that the word of the Lord in thy mouth is truth"*. The supernatural provision did not totally convince her he was a man of God and that he spoke truth.   But it was the ability to BRING LIFE, WHERE THERE WAS DEATH!

Praying according to Pattern is actually moving in the spirit of prophecy. Revelation 19:10 states, *"the testimony of Jesus is the spirit of prophecy"*.   So it shall be, that those speaking with the prophetic voice of the Lord, testifying of Jesus from the front gate to the Holy of Holies, will be heard and God will bring life where there was death all over the world!

Showdown At Mount Carmel

I Kin 18:1
And it came to pass after many days, that the word of the LORD came to Elijah in the third year, saying, Go, shew thyself unto Ahab; and I will send rain upon the earth.

In the third year of drought, Elijah is told by the Lord to present himself to Ahab, and He will bring rain upon the earth (James 5:17).   In I Kings 18:19-24, Elijah presents himself to Ahab and instructs him to have all the prophets of baal and the children of Israel to gather at Mount Carmel.   He then begins to reason with the Israelites, in an effort to bring them to repentance.

To end all dispute, Elijah called for two bullocks to be sacrificed and then declared the god that answered by fire would be God.   Everyone agreed to those terms and the prophets of baal worked in vain to get their god to answer.   But a god that does not hear, speak or see cannot answer (I Kings 18:26-29).

The Evening Sacrifice

Elijah repaired the altar that had been torn down (I Kings 18:30-32).   The *"apostolic-prophetic"* anointing will always repair that which was torn down and bring restoration of that which was lost. In repairing the altar, he used twelve foundation stones symbolic of the twelve sons of Jacob. Elijah was ACTING AS A PRIEST, restoring "true worship" for all of Israel! The sacrifice was prepared and covered three times with four barrels of water (I Kings 18:33-35). The number three is always prophetic of the Godhead, the Father, Son, and Holy Spirit and our praise and worship must include them all. Water is symbolic of the Word and we must water our sacrifice of praise with the Word, if we expect God to respond with His fire. In all, there were TWELVE barrels of water representing the apostolic fullness of the Word that will bring the fire!

The prophets of baal tried from morning until the time of the evening sacrifice. The evening sacrifice in the Temple at Jerusalem was 3:00 p.m. It was at this appointed time Elijah was to offer his sacrifice. He was observing the order in Jerusalem! Then Elijah prayed to the only true God and He answered by fire, the people fell on their faces and began to worship declaring *"the Lord He is God"*.

I Kin 18:37-39
HEAR ME, O LORD, HEAR ME, THAT THIS PEOPLE MAY KNOW THAT THOU ART THE LORD GOD, AND THAT THOU HAST TURNED THEIR HEART BACK AGAIN. Then the fire of the LORD fell, and consumed the burnt sacrifice, and the wood, and the stones, and the dust, and licked up the water that was in the trench. And when all the people saw it, they fell on their faces: and they said, THE LORD, HE IS THE GOD; THE LORD, HE IS THE GOD.

Elijah then purged and redeemed the land by killing the false prophets of Jezebel. *"And Elijah said unto them, Take the prophets of Baal; let not one of them escape. And they took them: and Elijah brought them down to the brook Kishon, and slew them there"* (I Kings 18:40).

To review so far; on Mount Carmel there was a blood sacrifice, repentance, turning back to the Lord in true worship and redeeming of the land. Mount Carmel, which means a fruitful field, garden and orchard could now live up to its name. In our season, praying according to Pattern or remembering the Law of Moses will create powerful sacrifices of praise that will manifest the presence of God. It will also destroy demonic forces and redeem the land so that it can bring forth the fruit of the earth!

The Sound Of Abundance Of Rain

I Kin 18:41-45
And Elijah said unto Ahab, Get thee up, eat and drink; for there is a SOUND OF ABUNDANCE OF RAIN. So Ahab went up to eat and to drink. And Elijah went up to the top of Carmel; and he cast himself down upon the earth, and put his face between his knees, And said to his servant, Go up now, look toward the sea. And he went up, and looked, and said, There is nothing. And he said, GO AGAIN SEVEN TIMES. And it came to pass at the SEVENTH TIME, that he said, Behold, there ariseth a LITTLE CLOUD OUT OF THE SEA, LIKE A MAN'S HAND. And he said, Go up, say unto Ahab, Prepare thy chariot, and get thee down, that the rain stop thee not. And it came to pass in the mean while, that the heaven was black with clouds and wind, and there was a great rain. And Ahab rode, and went to Jezreel.

This drought was caused by the Israelites forsaking the Law of Moses and their covenant. However, it was repentance, cleansing by the blood, and a return to true worship that produced the abundant rain of God's blessings. Elijah's servant looked seven times before the cloud appeared, while Elijah was praying. This is a prophetic picture of what the Father is doing in His people. We have Elijah whose name means *"beloved of Yah"*. *"Yah"* is our covenant God, so Elijah is a prophetic type of Jesus. He is sending forth the Holy Spirit, His Servant, to look *"SEVEN"* times towards the *"sea"* for the cloud, a sign of rain. The *"sea"* is symbolic of the people of God. Jesus our High Priest is interceding for us and the Holy Spirit is moving upon God's people desperately searching for true worshippers who will produce the true worship cloud so He can bring the rain!

The number *"seven"* always denotes perfection or completeness. The Tabernacle Prayer has seven steps to enter into the Holy of Holies! THE PERFECTION OF PRAYER WAS NEEDED TO PRODUCE THE WORSHIP CLOUD FOR THE RAIN! We cannot produce a "perfect" worship cloud in the Outer or Inner Courts, but only in the Holy of Holies as we worship at the Mercy Seat! The cloud was described as a little cloud like a man's hand, which is the worship cloud coming out of king-priests! Glory to God! It is the perfection of prayer that will produce all, from the fullness of the Saints, to the fullness of the harvest. It is the divine order of prayer that will accomplish all of these things!

Elijah's Journey

I Kin 19:8
And he arose, and did eat and drink, and went in the strength of that meat forty days and forty nights unto Horeb the mount of God.

After this great wave of anointing lifted, Elijah was running from Jezebel because she threatened to kill him. He also asked the Lord to take his life (I Kings 19:1-6). Elijah was a true servant of God, who knew his limitations. Like Elijah, we all should come to the realization that without the presence and power of God we can do nothing. The Lord supernaturally fed him and he journeyed across the wilderness to Mount Horeb. This was in the mountains of Sinai where Moses received the Law, statutes and the Tabernacle pattern. God is telling us in so many different ways to return to His divine order! *"Remember ye the law of Moses my servant, which I commanded unto him in Horeb for all Israel, with the statutes and judgments"* (Malachi 4:4).

I Kin 19:12-13
...and after the fire a STILL SMALL VOICE. And it was so, when Elijah heard it, that HE WRAPPED HIS FACE IN HIS MANTLE, and went out, and stood in the entering in of the cave. And, behold, there came a voice unto him, and said, WHAT DOEST THOU HERE, ELIJAH?

God asked Elijah *"What are you doing here?"* Elijah was in a cave rehearsing his problem to the Lord. He told God that he had been very zealous for Him, but the Israelites had forsaken His covenant, killed His prophets and he was the only one left and in danger of losing his life (I Kings 19:10).

The Lord told Elijah to stand upon the mountain before Him. According to I Kings 19:11-12, there was a wind, an earthquake and fire. And we are told the Lord was not in any of these things. But after the fire there was a *"still small voice"*. Elijah only came out of the cave when he heard the *"still small voice"* of the Holy Spirit. When he came out, he was wrapped in his mantle. This mantle was a prayer shawl called the *"tallit"*.

In Hebrew the word *"mantle"* means a garment that signified prayer that is glorious, powerful, and excellent and it also symbolized the Tabernacle of Moses! Moses instructed the children of Israel to make this garment as a reminder of their covenant (Numbers 15:38-39). The Jews would wear it across their shoulders and when they wanted to pray they would place it over their heads and it became a mini-tabernacle in which to pray and worship the Lord. *ELIJAH RESPONDED TO THE VOICE OF THE HOLY SPIRIT AND HE CAME OUT WRAPPED IN HIS MINI-TABERNACLE THAT SYMBOLIZED THE GLORY, POWER AND EXCELLENCE OF PRAYER!*

Now let's look at the big picture, here we have Elijah in the place where Moses received the Law, the statutes, and the Tabernacle pattern from God. Then we have the Holy Spirit asking him the most powerful question. The Holy Spirit is asking each one of us the same question, which is in reality a wake-up call, *"WHAT ARE YOU DOING HERE?"* When we respond to that wake-up call by becoming the king-priests of the Lord, we will fulfill our destiny!

The Anointing Of Elisha

God tells Elijah to anoint three people to bring about his judgment (I Kings 19:15-18). He said that whoever escaped the sword of Hazael, Jehu would slay. Whoever escaped the sword of Jehu, Elisha would slay. God chose at this point to tell Elijah that He had reserved 7,000 in Israel that had remained loyal to Him. We see the number *"seven"* again. God had a perfect remnant that would assist in destroying the enemy. Just as it is today, God has a remnant of king-priests who will bring about the destruction of all God's enemies by praying according to Pattern.

Let's take a look at the anointing of Elisha:

I Kin 19:19
So he departed thence, and found Elisha the son of Shaphat, who was plowing with twelve yoke of oxen before him, and he with the twelfth: and Elijah passed by him, and cast his mantle upon him.

The name *"Elisha"* means God of supplication and riches and also strength and might. *"Shaphat"* means to judge or execute judgment. Elisha, the son of Shaphat, represents divine prayer that is rich, full of power, and executes the judgment of God! Notice that Elisha was plowing when Elijah cast his mantle upon him. Plowing is prophetic of sowing the seed of the Word of God. You know God could have chosen to replace Elijah with an established prophet from the school of the prophets, but He chose a "SOWER"! As king-priests we "SOW" the Word of God into the earth. And as Jesus explains in Mark 4:14; *"The sower sows the Word"*, this is how the kingdom of God operates! Praise God for his manifold wisdom! It also states that Elisha was with the twelfth yoke of oxen. The number TWELVE represents duplication and to accumulate. It is also the number of divine government and apostolic fullness! When we pray according to Pattern, we sow the Word of God; execute judgment and duplicate king-priests to bring in the end-time harvest of souls.

At Mount Sinai God asked Elijah, *"What are you doing here?"* Isn't it interesting that after Elijah discovered what his purpose was, the next thing we see him *"doing"* is casting his prayer shawl (mini-tabernacle) upon Elisha and anointing him? He DUPLICATED HIMSELF in Elisha! It is also important to note Elisha's name represents POWERFUL PRAYER TO DEFEAT THE ENEMIES OF THE LORD! Once we enter our king-priest ministry and duplicate ourselves, we will utterly destroy the enemies of the Lord!

The Pathway Of Elijah

There were four places that Elijah and Elisha went before Elijah was taken to heaven (II Kings 2:1-6). Gilgal, Bethel, Jericho and Jordan are prophetic of our calling as king-priests. GILGAL means to commit, remove, roll away, and to trust. We must commit ourselves to our holy calling to pray in divine order and remove all prior traditions so we can obey the Lord.

When we learn to do these things in our relationship with Him, we are ready to go to Bethel. BETHEL means the House of God or Temple. There is no way around it, we must pray according to the divine order God has set in His House. It also means to begin to build, obtain children, repair, and set up. When we pray according to Pattern, we will build the House of God, duplicate ourselves and set up the Kingdom of God upon this earth.

JERICHO is the third stop, and it means to blow, perceive, touch, and make of quick understanding. God will do a quick work in these last days, bringing

His sons to maturity by the power of the Holy Spirit. This will take place if we create the proper atmosphere through prayer. And we do this by declaring the Word of God over them, so they will be able to receive. The last place is JORDAN, which means to bring down (abundantly), put down, subdue, and take down. This is warfare! As previously illustrated, God has provided the safest and most powerful way to do warfare in His House of Prayer. When we perform warfare in this way, which is simply praying in divine order, we will completely subdue and destroy our enemies!

In II Kings 2:9-10, Elisha asked for a double portion of the anointing that was upon Elijah. Elijah said, in essence, if you *"SEE ME GO"*, you will receive your request. When Elisha saw him leave he declared *"my father, my father, the chariot of Israel, and the horsemen thereof"*. The word *"chariot"* means a vehicle, team and army. The word *"Israel"* means those who will rule as God having power with God and man. The *"horsemen"* means a driver of the chariot or army who will separate, wound, scatter, declare and sting. In essence, it means an army that will have the power of God to destroy demonic forces! Elisha received the PRAYER MANTLE of Elijah and the double-portion anointing to ride upon the High Places and destroy demonic forces in the heavenlies.

If we can SEE THE TRUTH of our covenant to be king-priests unto God, we will also receive the mantle of Elijah and a double portion of the apostolic-prophetic anointing. This anointing will turn us into *"Elijahs"* who will ride upon the High Places of the earth destroying the enemies of the Lord, preparing the way for His Second Coming!

The Elijah Anointing

As you can see from this prophetic parallel of Elijah, drought conditions are produced by idolatry and forsaking of the covenant. But when the divine order of the Law of Moses is adhered to, which is true repentance, cleansing by the blood, and true worship, there will be restoration and the rain of God's blessings will be abundant.

As discussed earlier, Jeroboam stopped the celebration of the Feast of Tabernacles for the Northern kingdom. He instituted a counterfeit feast, with false gods, and led the Israelites into idolatry (I Kings 12:26-33).

The Jews had two very interesting rituals that marked the Feast of Tabernacles. At the height of the Feast, the High priest would POUR WATER ON THE BASE OF THE ALTAR, symbolizing worshipping God for the rain needed for the harvest (John 7:37-39). The second ritual involved all the Jewish people coming to the Temple area lifting up LIGHTED TORCHES! For miles the lighted torches could be seen all along the countryside (John 8:12). This symbolized worshipping God for the sunshine needed for a successful harvest! We see in the Gospel of John, Jesus was making prophetic declarations about Himself at both events. With Elijah, we see water poured at the base of an Altar and then we see God's fiery Torch coming down! Glory to God! WHAT ELIJAH ACTUALLY HAD DONE, WAS TO BRING THE ISRAELITES INTO A CELEBRATION OF THE FEAST OF TABERNACLES!

They were brought back to the true worship of the Lord. It is this Feast that is symbolic of the rain and final harvest. SO ONCE THEY HAD THEIR COVENANT OF TRUE WORSHIP RESTORED, THEY WERE READY FOR THE RAIN!

Again, we want to emphasize that *"remembering the Law of Moses"*, the *"Elijah Anointing"*, will precede this end-time Glory. When we become like Elijah, realizing our covenant and holy calling, we become *"beloved of Yah"*. By this we understand that we are in covenant with God and His provision for us will never fail. We remember His Word and our covenant by declaring them and testifying of the Lord Jesus Christ all the way through the Tabernacle.

The Lord's response will be to hear the voice of the prophetic and bring life out of death, thereby convincing the world that God is in us! As we approach Him according to His divine order, we gain the ability to walk in such close fellowship and intimacy with the Lord that we can freely come and go in and out of His presence. We are transfigured as we ascend into the holy mountain of God according to Pattern. We also have the power to confront demonic forces with the apostolic-prophetic anointing and bring them down in the name of Jesus!

As we stand in the gap and repent for the world, we apply the Blood of Jesus to all in prayer. This type of intercession turns their hearts to the Father bringing them to repentance. As king-priests, praying in divine order, we bring them into true worship unto the Lord.

Please understand that Elijah needed the PERFECTION OF PRAYER for the rain to come and so do we! The *"SON"* of God heats the *"living water"* within us, when we pray and worship in perfection. The vapors are then released to form a cloud of worship. The cloud shaped like a man's hand is symbolic of the "five-fold anointing" coming to perfection in king-priests. This worship cloud will produce an abundance of rain, which is needed for the end-time harvest of souls. The *"Elijah Anointing"* gives us great power to declare and decree the Word of God from the High Places, manifesting His purposes and His Glory upon the earth!

Joel 2:23

Be glad then, ye children of Zion, and rejoice in the LORD your God: for he hath given you the former rain moderately, and he will cause to come down for you the rain, the former rain, and the latter rain in the first month.

James 5:7

Be patient therefore, brethren, unto the coming of the Lord. Behold, the husbandman waiteth for the precious fruit of the earth, and hath long patience for it, until he receive the early and latter rain.

The Tabernacles, Temples, And Patriarchs

Temples Of God

The Word of God gives us four wonderful patterns of the Tabernacle and Temples of God. Each one provides great insight into how His Glory will be manifested upon the earth.

The Tabernacle Of Moses – Foundation Of True Worship

As described in detail before, the Tabernacle of Moses is the foundation for the worship of God. God delivered the Israelites from Egypt that they might come out of idolatry and learn how to worship Him as He desired.

Ex 3:10-12
Come now therefore, and I will send thee unto Pharaoh, that thou mayest bring forth my people the children of Israel out of Egypt. And Moses said unto God, Who am I, that I should go unto Pharaoh, and that I should bring forth the children of Israel out of Egypt? And he said, Certainly I will be with thee; and this shall be a token unto thee, that I have sent thee: When thou hast brought forth the people out of Egypt, ye shall SERVE GOD UPON THIS MOUNTAIN.

Their deliverance was not complete until they "SERVED" God on the mountain. Moses spent forty days in the presence of God on Mount Sinai. He received the Ten Commandments, the Law and statutes, the Tabernacle design, the Priesthood and all instructions on how to celebrate the Feasts.

Ex 19:4-6
Ye have seen what I did unto the Egyptians, and how I bare you on eagles' wings, and brought you unto myself. Now therefore, if ye will obey my voice indeed, and keep my covenant, then ye shall be a peculiar treasure unto me above all people: for all the earth is mine: And ye shall be unto me a KINGDOM OF PRIESTS, AND AN HOLY NATION. These are the words which thou shalt speak unto the children of Israel.

From the beginning, God has always wanted a nation of kings and priests. Adam functioned as a king and priest, having complete dominion and authority. God wanted Israel to be His nation of kings and priests. And the divine order for this ministry was given to Moses.

The Tabernacle Of David – Foreshadows The King-Priest Ministry

David acted as a king and priest, in bringing the Ark to his Tabernacle. And there is a mystery that is waiting for us to discover within the Tabernacle of David. God promises to raise it up in the last days.

Amos 9:11-12
In that day will I raise up the tabernacle of David that is fallen, and close up the breaches thereof; and I will raise up his ruins, and I will build it as in the days of old: That THEY MAY POSSESS THE REMNANT OF EDOM, AND OF ALL THE HEATHEN, which are called by my name, saith the LORD that doeth this.

The main reason that God desires to raise up the Tabernacle of David is so that we may "POSSESS" our inheritance, which are the heathen nations coming to Christ. When we discuss the restoration of the Tabernacle of David, we mean the spiritual significance of restoring the Davidic order of worship. David, as king and priest following divine order, brought the Ark to Mount Zion. Likewise, the manifest presence of the Lord in the forthcoming revival will be brought in upon the shoulders of the New Testament king-priests!

Mount Zion, where the Ark rested, was a hill in Jerusalem whose ancient name was Hermon. In the Old Testament, the word *"Zion"* means a permanent capital, a monumental guiding pillar, and a goal or something bright at a distance that we should travel towards. Furthermore, it means to be a superintendent of the Temple services and its music. In the New Testament, *"Zion"* means perpetual, constant, strength, victory, and the Church militant and triumphant.

When we combine these definitions, it is obvious that they describe both earthly and heavenly Zion. Earthly Zion was where David set up his king-priest government, which foreshadowed the ministry of Jesus. The Lord

Jesus Christ came as a King-Priest after the order of Melchizedek to establish our way into spiritual or heavenly Zion -- into the very presence of God! Heavenly Zion or heavenly Jerusalem is the city of God according to Hebrews 12:22, and of course it is a permanent guiding pillar, a bright goal that we should travel towards! We travel to spiritual or heavenly Zion by praying in the Pattern of the Tabernacle of Moses and worshipping in the Pattern of the Tabernacle of David. We then come forth as the victorious Church, militant and triumphant! Glory to God!

Another reason why God desires to restore the Tabernacle of David, the Davidic order of worship, is that God wants to restore the perfection of worship to the Church. In the Tabernacle of Moses, only the High Priest once a year had access to the presence of God. While in the Tabernacle of David, a number of priests had access to the presence of God twenty-four hours a day and there was continuous worship before the unveiled Ark. It is God's desire that we ALL have access to His presence!

Another undeniable factor in Davidic worship is that David had both Tabernacles operating simultaneously. First Chronicles 16:39-40, tells us that burnt offerings were continually offered, morning and evening, at the Tabernacle at Gibeon. It also states that they continued to do all that was written in the Law of the Lord. This illustrates that it is important to have the DIVINE ORDER OF PRAYER and approach to God, as in the Tabernacle of Moses, and the DIVINE ORDER OF FREE FLOWING WORSHIP as instituted by David in his Tabernacle. When we pray and worship in this manner, we will manifest the presence of God and bring in the end-time harvest of souls!

Isa 2:2-3
And it shall come to pass in the last days, that the mountain of the LORD's house shall be established in the top of the mountains, and shall be exalted above the hills; and all nations shall flow unto it. And many people shall go and say, Come ye, and let us go up to the mountain of the LORD, to the house of the God of Jacob; and he will teach us of his ways, and we will walk in his paths: for out of Zion shall go forth the law, and the word of the LORD from Jerusalem.

These scriptures show us that in the last days many people will desire to come to the House of God; learn His ways and walk in His paths. When we embrace the Tabernacle Prayer our prayers and worship will go forth out of Zion with power!

The Temple Of Solomon – The House of Prayer

God has declared that His House is the Tabernacle or Temple. He also declares it is the House of Prayer! To receive a clear understanding of that statement, let's review Solomon's prayer given at the dedication of the Temple.

I Kin 8:27-30
But will God indeed dwell on the earth? behold, the heaven and heaven of heavens cannot contain thee; how much less this house that I have builded? Yet have thou respect unto the prayer of thy servant, and to his supplication, O LORD my God, to hearken unto the cry and to the prayer, which thy servant prayeth before thee today: That thine eyes may be open TOWARD this house night and day, even toward the place of which thou hast said, My name shall be there: that thou mayest hearken unto the prayer which thy servant shall make TOWARD this place. And hearken thou to the supplication of thy servant, and of thy people Israel, when they shall pray TOWARD this place: and hear thou in heaven thy dwelling place: and when thou hearest, forgive.

Understanding the Word "Toward"

It is very important to understand that the word *"toward"* in the Hebrew means near, with, about, according to, and after. THESE SCRIPTURES ARE STATING THAT WE ARE TO PRAY ACCORDING TO THE DIVINE ORDER OF THE HOUSE OF GOD! God's answer to Solomon's prayer below; clearly shows His desire for us to *"pray in and according to"* the divine order of God's House! And He also promised that His eyes and heart would be there continually.

I Kin 9:3
And the LORD said unto him, I have heard thy prayer and thy supplication, that thou hast made before me: I HAVE HALLOWED THIS HOUSE, which thou hast built, to put my name there for ever; and mine eyes and mine heart shall be there perpetually.

The next scripture is a call to intercession in this holy place, by God Himself.

II Chron 7:14-16
If my people, which are called by my name, shall humble themselves, and pray, and seek my face, and turn from their wicked ways; then will I hear from heaven, and will forgive their sin, and will heal their land. Now mine eyes shall be open, and mine ears ATTENT UNTO THE PRAYER THAT IS MADE IN THIS PLACE. For now have I chosen and SANCTIFIED THIS HOUSE, that my name may be there for ever: and mine eyes and mine heart shall be there perpetually.

The House of Prayer

In the New Testament, Mark noted that Jesus said all nations shall call His House the House of Prayer. Luke records that Jesus boldly said that HIS HOUSE IS THE HOUSE OF PRAYER!

Luke 19:46
Saying unto them, It is written, MY HOUSE IS THE HOUSE OF PRAYER: but ye have made it a den of thieves.

Let's take a look at what the book of Isaiah says concerning the House of God as the House of Prayer.

Isa 56:7
Even them will I bring to my holy mountain, and make them joyful in MY HOUSE OF PRAYER: their burnt offerings and their sacrifices shall be accepted upon mine altar; FOR MINE HOUSE SHALL BE CALLED AN HOUSE OF PRAYER FOR ALL PEOPLE.

Praise His wonderful name! The Tabernacle is the House of God and the House of prayer for all people!

The Temple of Solomon Versus The Tabernacle of Moses

The Temple of Solomon was a combination of the Tabernacle of Moses and the Tabernacle of David, which is prophetic of the New Testament Church. The Temple combined the divine order and entrance into God's presence with the Davidic order of worship.

The Tabernacle of Moses was a quiet place where the priests solemnly ministered unto the Lord. Only the High Priest, on the Day of Atonement could enter into the presence of God before the Ark. In the Tabernacle of David, he freely ministered in the presence of the Lord, although he was not from the priestly tribe of Levi. He also appointed Levite singers and musicians to worship before the unveiled Ark twenty-four hours a day.

The Temple of Solomon, in its splendor, displayed God's desire for the New Testament Church. God desires His Church to be anointed, wealthy and have the manifestation of the Glory of God. In the past the greatest amount of wealth ever amassed was housed in the Tabernacle and Temples of God, in particular the Temple of Solomon. God desires to release the end-time wealth so we can establish His covenant in the earth.

Solomon's Temple also shows God's desire to have a NATION OF KINGS AND PRIESTS by the multiplication of the dimensions of the Outer and Inner Courts, and some of the furnishings in the Inner Court. The Tabernacle of Moses had one of each piece of furniture. The Temple of Solomon had one Brazen Altar, one Molten Sea, ten Candlesticks, ten Tables of Shewbread, one Altar of Incense and one Ark of the Covenant.

The Molten Sea, which sat upon twelve oxen, corresponded to the Brazen Laver. The twelve oxen were symbolic of the apostolic power of the Word of God. The oxen were facing the four corners of the earth, denoting the end-time strength and power of the Word that will cover the earth. There were ten Candlesticks and Tables of Shewbread. Five Candlesticks and Tables were placed on the right side of the Inner Court and the other five were positioned on the left. The number "five" signifies the "grace" of God or the supernatural ability to become His witnesses and intercessors. We will shine forth with the Glory of God and have fellowship and communion with Him.

Notice there was only one Brazen Altar, denoting one perfect sacrifice, the Lord Jesus Christ. One place for the priests to wash; signifying, that the priesthood could only be cleansed and ready for service by being washed by the water of the Word. Only one Altar of Incense, indicating there is only one way to worship God, in spirit and in truth. Only one Ark of the Covenant, characterizing one God—the Father, Son and Holy Spirit!

In the Tabernacle of Moses the Ark contained three items, which were the Tables of the Law, the Golden Pot of Manna and Aaron's Rod that blossomed. But in the Temple of Solomon the Ark contained only the Tables of the Law. The absence of the Golden Pot of Manna and Aaron's Rod symbolized their prophetic fulfillment in Solomon. He was full of wisdom and knowledge and his kingdom blossomed in fruitfulness. However, the Law was still in the Ark because Jesus, the Word, had not yet come to write His laws upon his heart and in his mind. Solomon had not become a carrier of the indwelling presence of the Lord. But we, the Church, have a new and better covenant!

Heb 8:10-11
For this is the covenant that I will make with the house of Israel after those days, saith the Lord; I will put my laws into their mind, and write them in their hearts: and I will be to them a God, and they shall be to me a people: And they shall not teach every man his neighbour, and every man his brother, saying, Know the Lord: FOR ALL SHALL KNOW ME, FROM THE LEAST TO THE GREATEST.

The Tabernacles and Temples

The Tabernacle of Moses provides us with the divine order that is needed to receive and maintain the presence of God. The Tabernacle of David provides the free flowing worship! David introduced musical instruments and the entire nation of priests worshipped before the unveiled Ark. However most importantly, David showed us that it takes a king and a priest to bring in the Glory – the Ark of God's Presence. The first time he was dressed in his kingly attire and the Ark was on a new cart. And as we know, that ended in disaster and they had to take the Ark to Obededom's house. After David went back to the writings of Moses he discovered that there was a divine order that needed to be adhered to. He then put on his priestly robe and danced before the Ark which was now carried on the shoulders of the priests. This clearly foreshadows that it's going to take a king and priest to bring in the Glory of God!

Solomon's Temple shows us that combining the two; the divine order of Moses and the free flowing worship of David's Tabernacle will produce the glory and wealth needed to touch and change the world! Can you imagine the wealthiest person in the world responding like the Queen of Sheba, saying *"Your God is the only true God"?*

Last but not least, we have Ezekiel's Temple where the water will flow out of the Temple, ankle, knee, and loin deep. Then it becomes so great one would have to swim in it. Ezekiel 47 tells us, that everything that lives or moves and that is touched by this river shall be healed and live: and there shall be a very great multitude of fish --- God's harvest of souls!!!

We Are The Temple Of God!

1 Cor 3:16
Know ye not that ye are the temple of God, and that the Spirit of God dwelleth in you?

We are the Temple of God and we are not just some empty building. If we are the Temple of God, we have an Altar of Sacrifice, Brazen Laver, Lampstand and a Table of Shewbread. We also have an Altar of Incense and Holy of Holies with an Ark of the Covenant in it!

And we are to worship the Lord there. We are to repent and enter His gates with thanksgiving and His courts with praise. We thank Him for being the Lamb of God who took away our sins. Thank Him for being the Word made flesh sent to heal us and deliver us from all our destructions. Thank Him that He is the Light of the World and the Lord of Glory who sent His precious Holy Spirit to live in us and to lead and guide us! We also thank Him that He is the Bread and Wine from heaven. And through His resurrection, gave us the power to stand in the gap for all men and bring in His end-time harvest of souls! We thank our Lord Jesus for making our prayers a sweet smelling aroma unto the nostrils of the Father. We also thank Him that He is our Covenant God, the King of Glory, Who cannot and will not forsake us! And we have the joy of thanking Him every day that He made us the Temple of the Living God!

The Patriarchs

God gave each patriarch, Abraham, Isaac, Jacob, Moses, David, Solomon and Elijah a part in laying the foundation for our king-priest ministry. By studying the Patriarchs we will clearly see how God has used each one to build the way for us to fulfill our destiny to become the manifested sons of God!

Abraham

Abraham entered into a holy covenant with God to make us kings and priests and he sacrificed his son, Isaac. This covenant sacrifice provided the way for Jesus Christ, the Chief Cornerstone and Foundation of the House of God, to come forth. Yes, covenant love made the way for God to manifest His Son in the earth and sacrifice Him for the sins of the world. We, as New Testament king-priests, must offer our Father the sacrifice of praise in order to manifest Jesus, the Son of God in our lives!

Isaac

Isaac was Abraham's miracle child and the son that he sacrificed at God's direction. And we know God accepted the fact that Abraham had sacrificed Isaac in his heart, therefore He did not require his physical death. Isaac is the type of the *"living sacrifice"* and we are told to present our bodies as living sacrifices unto the Lord as our reasonable *"worship"* (Romans 12:1). Therefore, we are to die to ourselves and worship God in the manner in which He requires.

Jacob

Jacob received a prophetic dream that revealed the purpose for the House of God, to be the House of Prayer. Jacob's dream also reveals that prayer offered in divine order, as shown by the steps of the ladder, takes us into the presence of God and summons angelic power on behalf of all men.

Moses

Moses was given the Torah, which contains the pattern for the Tabernacle, God's dwelling place. The Tabernacle of Moses was and always will be *"The Eternal Model For the Worship of God"*. The Torah also contains the divine order of worship for the priesthood and the Feasts of the Lord. These truths that Moses received enabled the Glory of God to dwell upon the earth. As New Testament king-priests we are to build a spiritual Tabernacle so the knowledge of the Glory of God can cover the earth as the waters cover the sea!

David

The Ark of the Covenant was brought to Mount Zion when David entered his king-priest ministry. He placed the model of the Melchizedek order of king-priest ministry in the earth and Jesus came and fulfilled it. When we enter our king-priest ministry we will also bring in the presence of God like David did, for this end-time Glory!

Solomon

Solomon, the man of peace, was a type of the Prince of Peace, the Lord Jesus Christ. He built the Temple of God and worshipped in the divine order of the Tabernacle of Moses and the pattern of worship that David established. The Temple of Solomon, in its entire splendor, is prophetic of the apostolic fullness and glory of the New Testament Church, which is yet to come!

Elijah

Elijah was another prophetic type of our king-priest ministry. He was a prophet who operated as a king and priest unto God. He had the power to decree that there would be no rain and it was at his word that rain would return *(kingly)*. He brought the Northern kingdom of Israel to repentance and a renewal of their covenant with the Lord *(priestly)*. He showed us that restoration of our covenant of true worship will bring the rain of God's blessings and the harvest of souls will be glorious!

After briefly reviewing the most important aspects of their lives, we clearly see the correlation between their accomplishments and our holy calling as kings and priests! Praise God forever!

Heb 11:13,16

These all died in faith, not having received the promises, but having seen them afar off, and were persuaded of them, and embraced them, and confessed that they were strangers and pilgrims on the earth. But now they desire a better country, that is, an heavenly: wherefore God is not ashamed to be called their God: for he hath prepared for them a city.

Heb 11:39-40

And these all, having obtained a good report through faith, received not the promise: God having provided some better thing for us, that they without us should not be made perfect.

Uniting The World In Prayer

"The One New Man"

Uniting The World In Prayer

John 17:21-23
That they all may be one; as thou, Father, art in me, and I in thee, that they also may be one in us: that the world may believe that thou hast sent me. And the glory which thou gavest me I have given them; that they may be one, even as we are one: I in them, and thou in me, that they may be made perfect in one; and that the world may know that thou hast sent me, and hast loved them, as thou hast loved me.

When Jesus prayed this prayer He was talking about the Jews and Gentiles coming together as one. At that time there were no Christian denominations, just Jews and Gentiles! Jesus said that this unity would cause the world to know that God sent His Son!

The Jews were given the divine order of worship in the Torah (Tabernacle and the Feasts). However, many do not understand that Jesus is the fulfillment of the shadow pictures in the Torah. On the other hand, many Gentiles have received Christ as the Messiah, but know nothing about their Jewish heritage.

Jesus wants the Jews to understand that He is the Messiah and the fulfillment of the Torah and worship Him in that manner. He also wants Gentiles to take their knowledge of Him as Messiah and apply that to the divine order of worship He gave the Jews. This is the true meaning of the unity Jesus was talking about!

When we unite in this type of worship it will cause the WORLD to know that God sent His Son! As His Glory rests upon us, the world will also know that we are perfected in love and unity and the Father loves us with the same love He has for His Son. That is astounding! Glory to God! Praying according to Pattern will accomplish all of this!

Hidden in the Tabernacle of Moses is the power and ability to unite all in prayer, performing the desires of God's heart. We may all differ in doctrines but if we belong to God and honor His Word we can all come into agreement upon what Jesus accomplished as the fulfillment of the Tabernacle. This gives us all a basis for agreement whereby we can come together and worship the Lord in one accord. This will fulfill the following scripture, *"Till we all come in the unity of the faith, and of the knowledge of the Son of God, unto a perfect man, unto the measure of the stature of the fulness of Christ"* (Ephesians 4:13).

It is and always has been God's desire to bring us together as one (John 17:21). One day in prayer, I began to ponder the importance of praying according to Pattern. As the different benefits began to flow across my mind, I heard the Holy Spirit ask, *"Have you ever heard of an army that was not organized?"* That startled me because the Church is supposed to be the Army of God but to date we have no organization! In every army there is government, unification, and specific goals and objectives. With the Tabernacle Prayer Pattern, we can become the mighty Army of God. The divine order of the Tabernacle Prayer displays God's government. It also brings unification and by virtue of the declared Word of God establishes His objectives in the earth.

The Tabernacle Prayer Pattern is so unique and multi-faceted that it can be prayed in several different ways. A prayer leader can pray it alone while everyone else comes into agreement. You can also have two people alternate or you can have a group of people, with each person praying a section of the Tabernacle. Another way is to simply follow the leader, with each person adding scriptures applicable to that section. The ultimate level is our desire to bring the Church together, globally, through satellite. We would have each continent pray a section of the Tabernacle so that the entire Body of Christ, Jewish and Gentile Christians can come together and worship God as "ONE NEW MAN". When we unify as a royal priesthood sending up spiritual sacrifices (I Peter 2:5-9), WE WILL BECOME THAT HOLY HABITATION and His Glory will manifest and the world will know that God sent His Son, the Lord Jesus Christ!

Eph 2:15

Having abolished in his flesh the enmity, even the law of commandments contained in ordinances; for to make in himself of twain ONE NEW MAN, so making peace;

Eph 2:21-22
21 In whom all the building fitly framed together groweth unto an holy temple in the Lord: In whom ye also are builded together for an HABITATION OF GOD through the Spirit.

Pray With Us!

Ps 87
His foundation is in the holy mountains. The LORD loveth the gates of Zion more than all the dwellings of Jacob. Glorious things are spoken of thee, O city of God. Selah. I will make mention of Rahab and Babylon to them that know me: behold Philistia, and Tyre, with Ethiopia; this man was born there. And of Zion it shall be said, This and that man was born in her: and the highest himself shall establish her. THE LORD SHALL COUNT, WHEN HE WRITETH UP THE PEOPLE, THAT THIS MAN WAS BORN THERE. Selah. As well the singers as the players on instruments shall be there: ALL MY SPRINGS ARE IN THEE.

This Psalm reveals the awesome power for the salvation of souls within the Tabernacle Prayer. Verse 6 says that the Lord Himself shall count as He writes up the people! This shows that God records how many were born into the Kingdom of God by our king-priest ministry! Psalms 87 also tells of the love that God has for this type of prayer, and the power and glorious benefits that go with it. It begins by saying, *"His foundation is in the holy mountains"*, and this means that there is strength and power in Zion.

As we learned earlier, Mount Zion is the heavenly Jerusalem that we reach by praying according to Pattern. It is in this realm, the High Place of the Lord, where we have power to destroy our enemies. Verse 2 says, *"The LORD loveth the gates of Zion more than all the dwellings of Jacob"*. The *"dwellings of Jacob"* represent the Tabernacle of Moses, but Zion represents the fulfillment and perfection of worship into the presence of God. Zion is the matrix or birthing place for the desires of God's heart for all of mankind. That's why verse 3 adds, *"Glorious things are spoken of thee, O city of God!"*

To further prove this point verse 4 says, *"I will make mention of Rahab and Babylon"*. The words *"Rahab"* and *"Babylon"* mean the proud and the confused. Then it says, *"behold Philistia and Tyre"*. The word *"behold"* means to watch and to take notice. *"Philistia"* means to roll, and to wallow self. That is one of our covenant promises, that God will roll or entwine Himself with us to give us the power of the Almighty! *"Tyre"* means a rock, which represents God the Almighty, and the One that came to build the family and House of God. Then it adds, *"with Ethiopia"*, which means Cush, or children of Ham. In summary this Psalm is saying that prayer according to Pattern will transform and save the proud, the confused, or in general the heathen nations!

According to verse 5, many will be born into the Kingdom of God from prayer that goes forth from Zion! No wonder God loves Zion! This beautiful Psalm ends with verse 7 saying, *"all my springs are in thee"*. The king-priests of the Lord who ascend into Mount Zion will have the living waters of God to bring in the end-time harvest!

Please don't let another day pass! All of His springs are in you, but they will not flow out and transform a lost and dying world unless you enter into your covenant as a king-priest. It is our desire to see true worshippers cover the earth. If you have been touched by this study guide and have decided to enter into your holy calling, we would like to know. Please visit our web site and let us know you have embraced your king-priest ministry. We will one day fulfill our destiny to worship God in unity as "ONE NEW MAN"! The Body of Christ praying and worshipping according to Pattern can achieve this. Let's pray the eternal purposes of God according to Ephesians 4:13, *"Till we all come in the unity of the faith, and of the knowledge of the Son of God, unto a perfect man, unto the measure of the stature of the fulness of Christ".*

If you have never received Jesus Christ as your personal Lord and Savior, this is where you must begin. Please confess the following prayer out loud:

Dear Heavenly Father,

I come to You in the name of the Lord Jesus Christ. I repent of my sins and I ask for Your forgiveness. I now confess that Jesus is my Lord and Savior and I believe in my heart that He died for me and was raised from the dead. I ask You Jesus to come into my heart and live Your life through me. At this moment I believe that I am born again by an act of Your love, grace and mercy. Thank You for saving my soul. Amen.

Rom 10:9-10
That if thou shalt confess with thy mouth the Lord Jesus, and shalt believe in thine heart that God hath raised him from the dead, thou shalt be saved. For with the heart man believeth unto righteousness; and with the mouth confession is made unto salvation.

Numbers 6:24-26

The LORD bless thee, and keep thee: The LORD make his face shine upon thee, and be gracious unto thee: The LORD lift up his countenance upon thee, and give thee peace.

I Am The "Life"
That Brings The "Light"!

While darkness is covering the earth and the people that is true;
The "Light" will chase the darkness completely from view.
The darkness will disappear; it has to leave that's right;
Says The Eternal God; "I Am the 'Life' that brings the 'Light'!"

Jesus is the Light of the world; to follow Him decide;
The "Light of Life" will cover you; in Him you shall abide.
Hear My voice; I declare unto you, arise and shine;
For the glory upon you will show the world that you are Mine.

The brightness of the King of kings, I want to be seen upon you;
And the people will be drawn to Me, if you let My glory shine through.
Throughout the whole earth; I say, My glory you will see;
And the souls that are affected, for all eternity.

From the earth, the face of darkness; it shall be ripped apart;
You shall see and be radiant, and joy will swell your heart.
Praise, honor, and glory will be given unto Me;
For I will turn to you the people; the abundance of the sea.

Lift up your eyes, and you will see that from all around they come;
They gather together in one accord to receive Christ Jesus the Son.
The Blood of Jesus Christ will cleanse all who come, from sin;
With the purifying fire, of the Spirit of God within.

Yes, darkness is covering the earth and the people that is true;
But remember, the "Light" will chase the darkness completely from view.
The darkness will disappear; it has to leave that's right;
Says The Eternal God; "I Am the 'Life' that brings the 'Light'!"

For Zion's sake will I not hold my peace, and for Jerusalem's
sake I will not rest, until the righteousness thereof
go forth as brightness, and the salvation
thereof as a lamp that burneth.
Isa 62:1

The Tabernacle Prayer

1 The Gate – Repentance

FATHER WE REPENT AND CONFESS OUR SINS.

Father, have mercy upon us according to Your loving kindness and tender mercies and blot out our transgressions. Wash us from iniquity and cleanse us from sin. For against You and You only we have sinned **(Ps 51:1-4).** Father in the name of Jesus, we repent for every sin, known, unknown, omitted, and committed. We repent for unforgiveness and we release and forgive all **(Mark 11:25).** We ask You to cleanse us from secret faults and keep us back from presumptuous sins; and let them not have dominion over us: then we shall be upright, and innocent from the great transgression **(Ps 19:12-13).** Father, we thank You that Your Word says in **I John 1:9,** if we confess our sins, You are faithful and just to forgive us, and to cleanse us from all unrighteousness. Create in us a clean heart and renew a right spirit within us and let the words of our mouth and the meditation of our heart be acceptable in Your sight O Lord our strength and Redeemer **(Ps 51:10) -- (Ps 19:14).**

The Gate - Thanksgiving

FATHER WE ENTER YOUR GATES WITH THANKSGIVING.
[Our Father Which Art In Heaven, Hallowed Be Thy Name]

Father we praise You, hallow Your holy name, and thank You for Your love. Lord we praise You for Your mighty acts and we praise You according to Your excellent greatness **(Ps 150:1-2).** O Lord, our Lord how excellent is Your name in all the earth **(Ps 8:1)!** The name of the

Lord is a strong tower and the righteous run into it and are safe **(Prov 18:10).** O magnify the Lord with us, and let's exalt His name together **(Ps 34:3).** The Lord's name is to be praised from the rising of the sun to the going down of the same **(Ps 113:3).** Every day we will bless You Lord, and we will praise Your name forever and ever **(Ps 145:2).**

*(Continue to bless the Lord and give thanks
for all that He has done for you.)*

2 The Brazen Altar

FATHER, THANK YOU FOR THE BLOOD OF JESUS CHRIST.
[Thy Kingdom Come]

Father, thank You for loving us so much that You gave Your only begotten Son, that whosoever shall believe in Him should not perish but have everlasting life **(John 3:16).** He was wounded for our transgressions, He was bruised for our iniquities: the chastisement of our peace was upon Him; and with His stripes we are healed **(Isa 53:5).** Thank You Lord Jesus for blotting out the handwriting of the ordinances that were against us and taking them out of the way by nailing them to Your cross. In the process You defeated and triumphed over every evil power and made a show of them openly **(Col 2:14-15).** Father God, we thank You for the precious Blood of Jesus that was shed for the remission of all our sins. We plead and apply the Blood of Jesus to every part of our lives and every precious stone in our breastplate. **Gal 3:13** assures us that Christ has redeemed us from every curse over our lives, that we may partake of the blessings of Abraham. Thank You Lord Jesus for redeeming us by Your Blood and making us king-priests unto God to reign on this earth **(Rev 5:9-10).** Father we thank You that Your kingdom has come in our lives.

3 The Brazen Laver

FATHER THANK YOU FOR YOUR WORD.
[Thy Will Be Done]

Father, we thank You that **John 1:1** says, in the beginning was the Word, and the Word was with God, and the Word was God. **John 1:14** says that the Word was made flesh, and dwelt among us, (and we beheld His Glory, the glory of the only begotten of the Father), full of grace and truth. Jesus is the Word made flesh. Your Word is made flesh or manifested in our lives, as we establish Your Word upon this earth. Your Word is health and healing to all of our flesh **(Prov 4:22)**. Your Word is quick and powerful and sharper than any two-edged sword and is able to divide the soul and spirit, the joints and marrow, and discern the thoughts and intents of the heart **(Heb 4:12)**. Your Word is a lamp unto our feet, and a light unto our path **(Ps 119:105)**. We receive the blessings of **Deut 28:1-14,** because we hearken diligently unto Your Word. We thank You Father that we have been sanctified and cleansed with the washing of water by the Word of God **(Eph 5:26)**. Your Word is Your will, therefore let Your will be done in our lives.

(This is where you can add specific "Word" declarations concerning personal and corporate prayer objectives)

4 The Golden Candlestick

FATHER THANK YOU FOR THE ANOINTING OF THE HOLY SPIRIT.
[In Earth, As It Is In Heaven]

In **John 8:12** Jesus said, I am the Light of the world and he that follows Me shall not walk in darkness but shall have the light of life. Father thank You for the light of life, which is the anointing. Jesus is the "Light of the world" and He has caused us to be a reflector of that light, which will bring glory to our Heavenly Father **(Matt 5:14-16)**.

Acts 10:38 states, that God anointed Jesus of Nazareth with the Holy Ghost and with power: who went about doing good, and healing all that were oppressed of the devil; for God was with Him. We are also anointed with the Holy Spirit and we are born of God for the purpose of destroying the works of darkness **(I John 3:8).** Jesus said in **John 14:12,** he that believes on Me, the works that I do he shall do also and greater works than these. Thank You Lord for the anointing of the Holy Spirit and the gifts of the Spirit to do these greater works. We ask You, Holy Spirit, to flow through us as You purpose with Your gifts, the gift of faith, gifts of healing, working of miracles, word of wisdom, word of knowledge, discerning of spirits, tongues, interpretation of tongues, and prophecy **(I Cor 12:8-10).** We have the sevenfold anointing; the spirit of the Lord, the spirit of wisdom and understanding, the spirit of counsel and might, the spirit of knowledge, and of the fear of the Lord **(Isa 11:2).** Father, correct us, so that nothing will hinder Your power from flowing through us and we can bring forth pure and holy light. Father, we thank You for the Holy Spirit, Who brings forth Your power from heaven. We also thank You for allowing us to share Your light all over this world.

5 *The Table Of Shewbread*

FATHER WE STAND IN THE GAP AND REPENT FOR ALL. THANK YOU THAT JESUS IS THE BREAD OF LIFE AND OUR POWER TO DO BATTLE. WE SPIRITUALLY PARTAKE OF COMMUNION, PUT ON YOUR ARMOR AND INTERCEDE FIRST FOR YOUR PURPOSES AND THEN PRAY OUR OWN PETITIONS.
[Give Us This Day Our Daily Bread. And Forgive Us Our Debts, As We Forgive Our Debtors]

Father as we come to Your Table as king-priests and intercessors, we stand in the gap for the Jews, the entire Body of Christ, the unsaved, and for the leaders of this world **(Ezek 22:30).** We stand in the gap and repent for we have all sinned, transgressed Your laws, committed iniquity, shed innocent blood, operated in unforgiveness, and have done wickedly in Your sight. **I John 1:9** says, if we confess our sins, You are faithful and just to forgive us. Father forgive and cleanse us with the Blood of Jesus.   Father, as we spiritually partake of communion, the broken body and shed Blood of Jesus, we thank You that Jesus is the "Bread of Life".   His body and Blood is our nourishment, strength and power to be victorious over all works of the enemy. It is also the "Children's Bread of Deliverance", therefore we are delivered from every foe within and without.   We put on the whole armor of God according to **Eph 6:10-20.** We are strong in the Lord and in the power of His might.   The weapons of our warfare are not carnal but they are mighty through God for the pulling down of strongholds **(II Cor 10:4-5).**   You have given us authority to tread upon serpents and scorpions, and over all of the power of the enemy and nothing shall by any means hurt us **(Luke 10:19).**   We bind every strong man that is set against us and loose the Angel of the Lord to plunder their house and spoil their goods **(Matt 12:29).**   According to **II Tim 4:18,** Father we declare that You will deliver us from every evil work and preserve us for Your heavenly kingdom. We pray that the unsaved will come to know Jesus Christ as Lord and Savior **(Ps 2:8).**   We ask for the heathen nations as our inheritance and the uttermost parts of the earth as our possession.   We also pray for the fear of God to fall upon every leader all over the world, thereby bringing them to repentance.   We declare that Your people will lead a quiet and peaceable life in all godliness and honesty and the gospel of Jesus Christ will continue to spread unhindered all over the world **(I Tim 2:2).**   Father we ask that we receive the spirit of wisdom and revelation in the knowledge of You, that the eyes of our understanding are enlightened that we might know the hope of our calling and to know the surpassing fullness of Your love **(Eph 1:17-23 -- 3:14-21).** We pray for the peace of Jerusalem, peace within their walls and prosperity within their palaces and we seek their highest good **(Ps 122:6-9).**   Father, thank You for the blessing over our lives that You promised us for loving and praying for Israel **(Gen 12:3).** We pray that the Body of Christ will come into the unity of faith, unto the knowledge of the Son of God, unto a perfect man, to the measure of the stature of the fullness of Christ **(Eph 4:13).**

(You can now pray your own petitions)

6 *The Altar Of Incense*

**FATHER CLEANSE OUR HEARTS AND PERFECT
YOUR LOVE AND THE FRUIT OF THE SPIRIT
WITHIN US.**
*[And Lead Us Not Into Temptation,
But DeliverUs From Evil]*

Father create in us a clean heart, O God; and renew a right spirit within us **(Ps 51:10)**. Perfect Your love in our lives according to **I Cor 13**. We want the fruit of the Spirit to ripen in us **(Gal 5:22-23 - II Peter 1:5-8)**. We pray for love, joy, peace, longsuffering, gentleness, goodness, faith, meekness and temperance: balanced with the gifts of the Spirit **(I Cor 12:8-10)**. Father God, we bring You worship attitudes of spontaneity, honesty, transparency, brokenness, the sweet fragrance of Jesus, and covenant speech. We ask You to come into our hearts, and let the light of Your countenance purge away all that is not pleasing to You and deliver us from evil **(Ps 4:6)**. We bring to You our weaknesses, hurts, wounds, broken dreams and broken hearts. We cast all of our cares upon You for You care for us **(I Peter 5:7)**. **Heb 7:25** says that Jesus is able to deliver us and ever lives to make intercession for us. Jesus is the Apostle and High Priest of our profession and confession **(Heb 3:1)**. We thank You Lord Jesus for perfecting our prayers, worship, and all that concerns us **(Ps 138:8)**. We also ask You to take the coal and cleanse our lips, for life and death are in the power of the tongue **(Prov 18:21)**. Put a guard over our mouths so that we will say only Your words of peace and prosperity over ourselves and others **(Col 4:6)**. Father we thank You that we have a covenant relationship with You. We are blessed of God Most High, the possessor of heaven and earth and blessed be God Most High; that has delivered all of our enemies into our hand **(Gen 14:19-20)**.

7 The Ark Of The Covenant

**FATHER THANK YOU FOR LETTING
US COME INTO YOUR HOLY PRESENCE.**
*[For Thine Is The Kingdom, And The Power,
And The Glory, For Ever. A-Men.]*

You have shown us the path of life: in Your presence is fullness of joy; at Your right hand there are pleasures for evermore **(Ps 16:11)**. Daddy thank You for the precious Blood of Jesus that is speaking from the Mercy Seat, proclaiming greater things than that of Abel **(Heb 12:24)**. We are so grateful Daddy, that when You look at us, You do not see us, but You see Jesus. Daddy God, thank You for making us vessels that are filled with Your presence **(Col 1:27)**. Your Laws are written upon our hearts and in our minds **(Heb 8:10)**. We speak and declare the truth of Your Word. We have revelation knowledge, and bud, blossom and bring forth fruit in resurrection power. The fruit and the gifts of the Spirit are operating in our lives in perfect balance. We are like the Ark, golden vessels, filled with Your covenant promises and with Your glory **(Isa 60:1-3)**. We worship You, Daddy, as the Giver and the Source of all life. We worship You, Holy Spirit, and we thank You for being the lover of our souls, our Comforter and our closest friend. We worship You, Lord Jesus, for You are the King of Glory, the Lord of Hosts, Captain of heaven's armies, and the Lord strong and mighty **(Ps 24:7)**. We declare that Jesus is Lord, and His dominion is everlasting. For thine is the kingdom, the power and the glory for ever and ever, Amen.

Short Tabernacle Prayer

Our Father Which Art In Heaven, Hallowed Be Thy Name

Father we come to You in the name of Jesus, repenting of all of our sins. Wash us from iniquity and cleanse us from sin. We repent for sins known and unknown, sins of word, thought and deed, and also secret faults **(Ps 51:1-4).** Cleanse us according to **I John 1:9;** Your Word states if we confess our sins, You are faithful and just to forgive us and cleanse us from all unrighteousness. Father we enter Your gates with thanksgiving and Your courts with praise, exalting the name of Jesus which is above every name **(Eph 1:20-21).** We declare that Jesus is Lord over this day.

Thy Kingdom Come

Father we thank You that Jesus is the Lamb of God, Who shed His Blood for our sins and complete deliverance **(John 1:29 - John 3:16).**

Thy Will Be Done

Father, we also thank You that Jesus is the Word made flesh **(John 1:14)** and You sent Your Word to heal us and deliver us from our destructions **(Ps 107:20).** We also thank You for washing us by the water of Your Word so we can come forth as Your bride, holy and pure **(Eph 5:26-27).**

In Earth, As It Is In Heaven

We exalt You Father for the power and the anointing of the Holy Spirit, making us Your Lampstand **(Matt 5:14-16)**. We reflect Your light and walk in miracles, signs, and wonders.

Give Us This Day Our Daily Bread. And Forgive Us Our Debts, As We Forgive Our Debtors

Father we come to stand in the gap and repent for all mankind. We have all sinned and fallen short of Your glory and we ask for Your forgiveness **(Dan 9:5,19)**. As we spiritually receive communion, the broken body and shed Blood of Jesus, we gain full power to war, battle and overcome. We put on the whole armor of God and pray for every precious stone in our breastplate, the Lost, the Leadership, the Body of Christ and the Jewish Nation **(I Tim 2:1-4)**.

We declare that You will deliver us from every evil work and preserve us for Your heavenly kingdom – to You be the glory for ever and ever **(II Tim 4:18)**. We pray for the peace of Jerusalem, peace within their walls, and prosperity within their palaces **(Ps 122:6-9)**. Father, we thank You for the blessing over our lives that You promised us for loving and praying for Israel **(Gen 12:3)**. We thank You that we all come into the unity of faith perfected in Christ **(Eph 4:13)**.

And Lead Us Not Into Temptation, But Deliver Us From Evil

We come to You as true worshippers in the earth, worshipping You in spirit and in truth **(John 4:23-24)**. We purge our hearts and bring that perfect blend of heart motivations and attitudes **(Gal 5:22-23)**. We exalt Jesus the Apostle and High Priest of the House of God. He makes this prayer and our worship perfect before You and leads us into Your presence **(Heb 3:1)**.

For Thine Is The Kingdom, And The Power, And The Glory, For Ever. A-Men.

Father we come beyond the Veil into Your presence, worshipping at the Mercy Seat, Your throne of grace **(Heb 4:16)**. We worship You Father, Jesus the Lamb of God, and Holy Spirit in the joy of Your presence **(Ps 16:11)**. We exalt You, Father, and magnify Your name and the name of Jesus in all the earth. We love You and we thank You for loving us! For thine is the kingdom, the power and the glory forever! Amen **(Matt 6:13)**.

Model For Creating Your Own Prayer

1. **Repent**
    [Father We Repent And Confess Our Sins]

    _____

    _____

    _____

    Enter His Gates With Thanksgiving
    [Our Father Which Art In Heaven, Hallowed Be Thy Name]

    _____

    _____

    _____

    _____

2. **Thank God For The Blood Of Jesus Christ**
    [Thy Kingdom Come]

    _____

    _____

_____

_____

_____

_____

_____

_____

_____

_____

3.   Thank God For His Word
       [Thy Will Be Done]

_____

_____

_____

_____

_____

_____

_____

_____

_____

_____

4. Thank God For The Anointing Of The Holy Spirit
    [In Earth, As It Is In Heaven]

_____

_____

_____

_____

_____

_____

_____

_____

_____

_____

5. **Stand In The Gap, Repent, And Intercede For The World**
   [Give Us This Day Our Daily Bread. And Forgive Us Our Debts, As We Forgive Our Debtors]

_____

_____

_____

_____

_____

_____

_____

_____

_____

_____

6. **Purge Your Heart And Worship God In Spirit And In Truth**
    [And Lead Us Not Into Temptation, But Deliver Us From Evil]

_____

_____

_____

7.   **Worship The Father, Son, And Holy Spirit**
      [For Thine Is The Kingdom, And The Power,
      And The Glory For Ever. A-Men.]

_____

_____

_____

_____

_____

_____

_____

_____

_____

The Awesome Power Of God

Exam Questions

The Awesome Power Of God
Exam Questions

Date:_____

Name:_____

1. List at least (2) scriptures that prove you have a king-priest ministry.

   _____
   _____
   _____
   _____
   _____

2. List the basic meaning of each step in the divine order of the Tabernacle Prayer.
   1.
   _____
   1a.
   _____
   2.
   _____
   3.
   _____
   4.
   _____
   5.
   _____

6. _____

7. _____

3. What do the bells and the pomegranates on the hem of the priestly garment represent?

_____

_____

4. What are your duties as a king and priest?

_____

_____

5. Why is it important to repent before praying?

_____

_____

_____

6. What are the benefits of declaring the Word of God in prayer?

_____

_____

_____

7. Why didn't God accept Cain's sacrifice?

_____

_____

8. Why was Gethsemane important?

_____

_____

_____

_____

9. Where is the covenant promise to Abraham and the actual establishing of the covenant found in scripture?

_____

_____

_____

10. How does praying the pattern build faith?

_____

_____

_____

_____

11. What was the cover to the Ark of the Covenant called?

_____

_____

12. What does Jacob's Ladder prophetically represent?

_____

_____

13. What are the seven-fold mercies of the Blood and where is it found in the Bible?

1. _____

2. _____

3. _____

4. _____

5. _____

6. _____

7.

14. What produced the rain during the days of Elijah?

15. What important action did Jesus teach that correlates with the Pattern of the Tabernacle?

16. What are the (3) gates within the Tabernacle and in what scripture reference does Jesus proclaim them?
    1.

    2.

    3.

17. What are the promises God has given when we become one and what is the scripture reference?

18. What was the only day the High Priest of Israel could enter the Holy of Holies?

19. What are the (3) main Feasts of Lord and in what book, chapter and verses of the Bible are they explained?

1. _____

2. _____

3. _____

_____

20. How many loaves of bread were on the Table of Shewbread?

_____

21. On the priestly garment where were the names of the Tribes of Israel engraved?

_____

22. Where is David's repentance found after his sin?

_____

_____

23. Who was the first High Priest of Israel?

_____

24. Why did God give Moses the Tabernacle Pattern?

_____

25. Name the original priestly tribe.

_____

26. What (2) offices did Melchizedek hold?

_____

27. What scripture declares that God will cleanse us if we confess our sins?

_____

28. What common Christian practice is symbolized by the Table of Shewbread?

_____

29. List the Tabernacle furniture including the entrance and link to the corresponding phrase in the Lord's Prayer.
    1.

    _____

    2.

    _____

    3.

    _____

    4.

    _____

    5.

    _____

    6.

    _____

    7.

    _____

30. Who was Elijah's assistant?

_____

31. What building was a combination of the Tabernacle of Moses and David?

_____

32. In what scripture is the Abrahamic blessing found?

_____

33. Why is it important to pray for the peace of Jerusalem?

_____

_____

34. List the (5) main ingredients in the Anointing Oil.
    1.
    _____
    2.
    _____
    3.
    _____
    4.
    _____
    5.
    _____

35. List the (5) main ingredients in the Worship Incense.
    1.
    _____
    2.
    _____
    3.
    _____
    4.
    _____
    5.
    _____

36. What tribe was Jesus from?
    _____

37. What is the eternal ministry of Jesus?
    _____

38. What does the word repent mean?
    _____

    _____

39. List (1) scripture reference per step that applies to each piece of Tabernacle furniture including the entrance.
    1. _____
    1a. _____
    2. _____
    3. _____
    4. _____
    5. _____
    6. _____
    7. _____

40. How many sons did Jacob have?

    _____

41. Who was Jacob's father?

    _____

42. Name the (4) Tabernacles / Temples in our study.
    1.

    _____
    2.

    _____
    3.

    _____
    4.

    _____

43. Name (2) examples of intercessors from our study.
    1.

    _____
    2.

    _____

44. Name the (4) categories of people we pray for.
1.

_____

2.

_____

3.

_____

4.

_____

45. Who dreamed a prophetic dream about stairs?

_____

46. In what part of the Tabernacle does God commune with you?

_____

47. During what Feast was Jesus crucified?

_____

48. During what Feast was the Holy Spirit given to the Church?

_____

49. What Feast has not yet been fulfilled?

_____

50. What is your holy calling?

_____

King-Priests Releasing
The Awesome Power Of God

Did you know that you have a holy calling to be a king and priest unto the Lord? Yes, by the Blood of Jesus you have been made a king and priest and all creation is waiting for you to fulfill this holy calling! You have come to the kingdom for such a time as this to become one of the manifested sons of God! The mysteries revealed in this book are divine strategies from the throne of God to propel you into your final destiny as a king-priest and to manifest the Glory of God!

We are in the last of the last days, as we enter this season, we must enter into a new dimension of prayer. This prayer revolution is the catalyst for the shift needed to go to the next and final level. Most importantly, it will fulfill the desire of the Lord's heart to bring the Body of Christ into unity for the end-time harvest of souls and the glorification of the Saints.

You will be forever changed after being enveloped in the pages of these two books. They are both practical and insightful step-by-step books to teach you who you are and how to manifest The *Awesome Power Of God*" anywhere and at anytime!

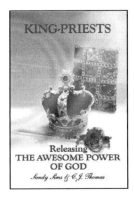 

Sharing The Light Ministries
P.O. Box 596
Lithia Springs, GA 30122
www.myholycall.com

In The KING'S Presence

The Lord called C.J. to enter His presence, know His heart, and share His heart with others. Her book of poetry is an inspiring collection of comforting and uplifting Christian poems. They are designed to glorify our Lord and Savior Jesus Christ and to inspire others to allow His anointed Word to change their lives. This poetry highlights God's grace and His matchless love, and is to be shared with everyone. You will know the heart of God as you determine to spend time, In The KING'S Presence!

"In The KING'S Presence"

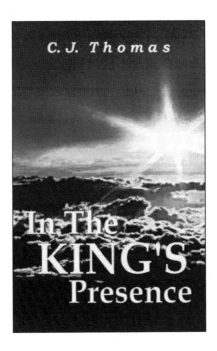

Visit web site: www.myholycall.com
Email: prayer@myholycall.com

8701315R0

Made in the USA
Charleston, SC
06 July 2011